Setting

the

Gospel

Free

Nicholas King SJ

Cluster Publications
1995

ISBN 1-875053-03-4

First published in 1995.

Published by Cluster Publications
P.O. Box 2400
Pietermaritzburg
3200
Republic of South Africa

Printed by The Natal Witness Printing and Publishing Company (Pty) Ltd

Contents

Lokhu wenzela uXolile Keteyi SJ
owasishiya ngomhlaka 31 ku Meyi 1994

Feast of the Visitation

Requiescat in Pace

Introduction

Setting the Gospel Free

In July and August of 1993, two of us, a French Catholic priest with a parish in Soweto, and myself, an English Jesuit teaching Scripture in Natal, South Africa, visited six different places in South Africa and neighbouring countries, giving lectures on "How to Read the Bible in Southern Africa Today". For both of us it was an extraordinarily exhilarating experience. It was a momentous time in the history of South Africa, a time of great change; and for my colleague in particular it was a sign of the dawn after a long night. For Emmanuel Lafont had been twelve years in this country, passionately committed to the struggle for freedom, so much so that he had on more than one occasion been arrested and threatened with deportation, and after all that time he still did not have the right of permanent residence in South Africa; so whenever we left the country, he had to make sure that he would be allowed back in.

For me too they were heady days; I had been in the country less than four years, and was certainly not living in Soweto, nor anything like it; but those four years had seen extraordinary changes, and extraordinary, and in my view utterly evil, resistance to those changes. The monster of an obviously unjust society was in its death-throes, although it was still thrashing about to some effect. There was therefore a combination of optimism and apprehension such as is entirely appropriate to a new and largely uncharted beginning.

In that context we were asking ourselves, and encouraging our audiences to consider, how one can read the Bible. What we encountered, and we should not perhaps have been surprised at this, was a passionate thirst for Scripture. This thirst was not however for the "Bible bingo" practiced by those Christians who think they have solved a problem by quoting a chapter and a verse from a Scriptural book. On the whole they longed for what they felt the Bible contained, but there were two further conditions: first, it had to draw on modern scholarly research into Scripture, and, second, it had to make sense in the context in which they lived. What people were looking for was a way of understanding what was going on, what God was doing in this society. Whether we succeeded in this you may in part judge from this book, which is principally based on the lectures I gave as we did our tour. We learnt as we went, and we debated often with each other and with those who came to the lectures; and we virtually always attended each other's lectures. Therefore it is quite likely that in the pages that follow there is material that I have stolen from Emmanuel Lafont. If so, that may be taken as a token of my great gratitude to him for what he taught me as we travelled.

There are other sources, as well, of course. I am living and working in Natal, which has been a troubled place; and occasional work in a Zulu parish, and a limited contact with ordinary Zulu people and their problems, is part of the background against which this book is written. My main work, however, is not that of a parish priest, but as a teacher in a seminary attended by mainly black students from all over Southern Africa. These students have won my admiration for their commitment and their readiness for the enormous task that is in hand, and they have given me some grasp of their problems of living in this country today.

Before teaching you have to study, of course, and for more than twenty years, I have been studying the Bible in a reasonably serious way; but I no longer see it as I did when I started to learn about the scientific study of Scripture. In those days, I think we thought that if you refined your methods, and increased the number of languages you could read, and ploughed through weighty tomes in German, you would eventually come to "the meaning of the text". I no longer believe that; it seems to me that the Bible is not an object of clinical study so much as a live and dangerous force that can address us today and in this country, that can challenge us and disconcert us and set us free and wonderfully enhance our lives.

For that reason you will find in these pages very many biblical references, and I should like you to read them with Bible in hand, checking my quotations, and verifying my references; for I might have made mistakes or argued incorrectly or let my eye slip on the page. I should like the reader to become fascinated by the Bible. It is more important that you should read the Bible than that you should read this book, though this book is written in the hope of helping people to discover the Bible's power. The quotations may sometimes appear unfamiliar: for Old Testament I have used the New Revised Standard Version, because I like it, while for New Testament I have made my own, sometimes deliberately tendentious, translation, with a view to bringing the reader up short and making her (or him) think a little.

What I am about here is a particular way of reading the Bible, namely through the eyes of the poor. I cannot pretend to be poor, except in the sense that I am a Jesuit priest vowed to religious poverty; my primary work is as an academic and therefore not directly with the poor. Inevitably, for Natal is that sort of place, there is some kind of contact with the poor, and the trick is to feel that contact as a constant challenge, and an invitation to life, rather than a destructive threat or a source of useless guilt.

The challenge comes, of course, from the God whom we encounter in a unique way in the pages of the Bible, and I have resisted (often with heroic restraint) the temptation to litter the pages that follow with footnotes. Anyone who knows the literature will immediately recognise my debt to a number of scholars; but I have not in this book made the debt explicit, because my emphasis is going to be all on the text of the Bible, and not on what has been written about it. There are many books to which you can go to find out what more to read; I should like the readers of this book to go back to the Bible as their first port of call.

Some acknowledgements must be made, however. I am grateful to the Editor of *Priests and People* for permission to use an article that I wrote for that excellent journal in December 1993, which is an earlier version of chapter 3. The quotation from the Dead Sea Scrolls in chapter 7 is taken from *The Dead Sea Scrolls Uncovered*, by Robert Eisenmann and Michael Wise. These two authors have performed a useful service to all scholars in offering transcriptions and translations of hitherto unpublished fragments from Qumran, even if their conclusions, and even some of their readings, will not command universal assent. Finally, a good deal of what I say in chapter 7 is shamelessly plagiarised from my friend Brendan Byrne SJ, whose admirable book *Paul and the Christian Woman* I commend to all readers.

The title that I have lighted upon is *Setting the Gospel Free*. This is slightly pretentious, I fear, but it is meant to convey three things. First, it implies that the gospel is free of constraints of time and space. Frequently in this book I shall speak of "today" and "this country", and mean by them the time and the place where you, the reader, read the book and, more importantly, the Bible. Secondly, it is meant to imply that the Bible is on the side of freedom and opposed to oppression of all sorts. Thirdly, I want also to convey something of the power of Scripture: it cannot be domesticated like a great religious pussy-cat, but will forever refuse to be chained by us human beings, and will always be tugging at the constraints we seek to put on it, until they snap and we are set free for new life.

Forethought

"Away with Solemnity" and "Back to the Text"

i) Away with Solemnity

Solemnity can be the most terrible enemy of true religion. A good example is that most solemn aberration, Docetism. Docetism, the doctrine that Jesus was not really human, but only seemed or pretended to be, was the earliest heresy in the Christian Church, and the Church's instinct has always been to resist it firmly. There is a similar process that goes on with Scripture. Because it is "Sacred Scripture" or "Holy Writ", or the "Good Book", it is to be uttered in those soupy tones beloved of the religious programmes on SABC, and listened to with bowed head and the dutiful response of "thanks be to God": the effect of this is to reserve it for Church, and to insulate it from real life, and so to remove from it its challenging rawness and humanity. When Scripture is put in the tabernacle in this way, or chained to the pulpit, paradoxically its effectiveness is reduced, in just the same way as a Jesus who is not really human lacks any relevance to our human plight.

It is my conviction that we need to restore the excitement to Scripture, to feel once again the hot blood that courses through its veins, to give up the "hushed voices" approach whose effect is to domesticate the gospel's wildness.

To do this we also need Scripture scholars to give up the "laboratory" approach, the assumption that was made when I received my theological education, that you can refine your techniques of scholarship further and further until eventually you come to the "objective meaning" or, it seemed at times, discover that there is nothing at all left. This is not to attack the work of Scripture scholars; we need all their techniques in order to get as close as possible to grasping the original conditions in which these texts were produced. It is, rather, to say that Scripture scholars need to get their sleeves rolled up and their hands dirty. Or, to put it another way, to allow the raw humanity of Scripture to appear, not only in its original context but also in the context of the reader whose life is presumably meant to be enhanced and challenged by it.

This means, I think, that scholars must learn to read their Bible contextually, and, in particular, "from below". For if we read it "from above" then we domesticate the gospel to a point where it is no longer good news because it is no longer challenging. And most Scripture scholars inevitably tend to read "from above", because of our background. I should say at this point that I do not really call myself a Scripture scholar, so much as an attentive reader; but the charge can be laid against me too. Once Scripture's raw humanity is lost, as can happen if you speak too readily or too uncritically of its being "inspired", then its divinity is also lost. Perhaps we should start a campaign to take the Bible (and God) out of church and read it under the trees, at the tops of mountains, by a fireside, in the townships of South Africa, and wherever people are having peak experiences of joy and suffering. For it is at these moments and to those people that the Bible speaks loudest. "Blessed are those who know their need of God" is a thought-provoking translation of Matthew's first beatitude: and primarily that means those nearest to despair, those who are suffering most. That means the poor, and there is no getting away from it.

That does not mean that you can simply read Socialism or Liberation Theology out of the Bible without any further ado, for they are human constructs too, and also need to be challenged. But it is possible to argue that they come closest to the Scripture's raw humanity.

Two elements that seem to me essential in reading the gospels in particular are those of *story* and *humour*. We have vaccinated ourselves against finding jokes in the Bible, but surely, even allowing for cultural differences we are supposed to roar with laughter at the picture in Matthew 7:3-5 of the man with a huge plank in his eye criticising his fellow for having a tiny speck? And as for story, some of the best stories in world literature are to be found in the Bible; and a story has at least three elements: a story-teller, a hero, or anti-hero, and an audience. Unless we are alert to these three elements, we shall miss what the story is supposed to do to us. For there is a story-teller, and it is the part of the scholar, or the attentive reader, to show us the story-teller's characteristics. Then there is a hero: God, or Jesus, or various other Biblical characters. And finally there is the audience. And gospel is not gospel until we, the audience, step aboard and make it our own story, what a colleague of mine terms a "fifth gospel", the one which we write in our own lives.

Now these two elements, of story and humour, are very common among the poor. There may be two reasons for this: firstly, neither of them costs very much, and, secondly, they both help people to cope with life. There is not, it must be said, much of either in socialism or liberation theology or academic theology. So my first slogan is "Away with Solemnity".

Does this mean that we are not to believe in the inspiration of the Bible? Not at all. Obviously we treat Scripture in a particular way because we regard it as special for us, as the Church's gift to itself; but that does not necessarily entail that we should get all solemn about it, as though a raucous laugh or a rush of blood might disturb the Holy Spirit as She whispers in the evangelist's ear.

ii) Back to the Text

Believers have, quite correctly, it seems to me, a sense that somehow "it's all there in the Bible". That is quite right, for the Bible is the Church's gift to itself, what the Church wants to say about God and about the significance of Jesus Christ. But it is of enormous importance that we look at what the text actually says, not what we think it ought to say, or what we have the impression it said last time we looked at it. For very often you will find yourself quite surprised by what it actually says; even today, after many years of fairly attentive reading of the Bible, I find myself surprised by texts that I thought I knew quite well. And not just surprised, but also challenged, because for Jewish and Christian believers the Bible carries in human words the Word of God, which is permanently new and permanently challenging, breaking down our comfortable certainties, and pushing us to the edges of human language.

So it is "back to the text"; but that is not as simple as it sounds, and I'd like to address various questions that people often ask when they start thinking about what it might mean to get "back to the text" of the Bible.

a) What text?

The Bible was written in Hebrew and Aramaic and Greek, and not everyone can wrestle with those languages. Most people therefore have to read the Bible in their own language, which in the case of most people reading this book will be English. And very often people make the calm assumption that the Bible was written in English, at the dictation of an anglophone Holy Spirit. Sadly, that is not quite the case. Now does the fact that it was not written in our own native language mean that we can't get back to the text? Not at all, for God speaks to us through even the uninspired work of human translators; but we need to remember that we are dealing with intermediaries who would certainly not claim divine inspiration. And that is true even if we *can* read the biblical languages, for we are still at the mercy of those who copied the texts down the centuries, since in no case do we have the original manuscripts. All we can say is that the Church, that is to say the community of believers, has given us these copies and these translations. So it is perfectly acceptable to read the Bible in translation; but let me recommend that you have at least two different versions to hand, and use them simultaneously, checking one against the other, to get the fullness of meaning of God's word.

b) Which versions of the Bible should you use in English?

Well, all of us have our prejudices, and all of us have our pet aversions. I suggest, as I say, that you should really have at least two copies of the Bible, and that one of them should be your favourite version, the one you feel most at home with, and one of them should be a modern, scholarly edition, one of those ones with useful notes.

c) How should we read the Bible?

That is really what this book is about. In a way, though, it doesn't matter, provided you do actually *read* the Bible, provided you do not start by thinking (as we humans tend to do) that you already know all the answers, and provided you are prepared to be challenged by the text. The more you read and reread the text, the more surprises you will find, the more you will find yourself asking: "what is God really saying to me and to us today?" For it is of the nature of God, ever old and ever new, permanently to challenge us.

d) What does it mean to say that "God speaks to us today in the biblical text"?

This can be a tricky question, for obviously the biblical text was written by human beings, with all their limitations, who lived not less than nineteen centuries ago, and perhaps as many as three thousand years ago. Any text has, however, a certain life of its own, independent of its author, and the fact is that people today can still hear the voice of God speaking to them and challenging them. It is not, let me hasten to add, a matter of thumbing through the Book of Revelation, and discovering that the world will end a week next Tuesday. And, by the way, if you think that is a frivolous example, then just watch the number of hairy characters who will be producing copies of the Bible as we come nearer to the beginning of the third millenium, and loudly proclaiming that The End of The World is Nigh, and that you will be safe if and only if you follow them and their teachings up the nearest mountain. Rather, the idea that God speaks to us today in the biblical text is a matter of a calm conviction that if we listen prayerfully to the Bible as a whole, then the unmistakable accents of the voice of God will be heard. As a matter of fact, I think that it is quite legitimate to do the equivalent of what was known in Latin as the Sortes Virgilianae, opening a page of the Roman poet Virgil at random, to be guided by whatever lines should leap to the eye. For example, as a Catholic priest, I have to pray through each day a fairly sizeable chunk of the "breviary", a collection of psalms, scripture and other readings, and prayers of various kinds, and it is astonishing how frequently a text comes up that exactly speaks to my mood, whether angry or frustrated or peaceful or exultant. That, it seems, to me, may legitimately be regarded as God speaking to us. What is not legitimate is to play the game of Biblical Bingo, the rules of which are that I quote various biblical texts in order to prove that I am right and you are wrong.

e) What about the biblical "experts"?

"Experts" are very intimidating animals, and sometimes we can imagine them looking over our shoulders disapprovingly, and saying "you can't possibly read the Bible like that", and so we get paralysed with fear, and feel we cannot open Scripture and read a single sentence without first submitting our interpretation to higher authority. Now we need our experts; biblical scholars can shed a great deal of useful light on the context in which our texts were written, and can help us to establish the meaning of difficult passages, what the author might have intended to say. It is of the greatest importance that there should be scholars in all branches of Christianity and Judaism who can help deepen our understanding of what is going on in the Bible. It is enormously stimulating for any reader to learn from the literary and linguistic and other skills of Scripture scholars. Sometimes we can get a bit of a shock from what the scholars say. Occasionally that will be because like the rest of humanity they can enjoy shocking; sometimes it will be because that is the way God operates with us. So it is quite proper to allow ourselves to be questioned and challenged by the experts, and, of course, we in turn may properly question and challenge them. For being an "expert" does not mean you are right, as you will know if ever you have heard extremely competent Scripture scholars disagreeing with each other. On any passage at all you will find experts with widely differing views. That does not mean that we can never discover the meaning of a particular text, only that we never come to the end of the depths of the mystery of God. All the time, the experts will call us, and perhaps this is their real function, "back to the text".

f) What about the poor?

Again and again in the texts of the Old and New Testaments, if you keep your eyes open, you will find the deep-rooted belief that God is on the side of the poor and the marginalised. That is what going "back to the text" can mean for us. And it is very good for us. It is worth noticing that if you are reading this book, you are probably not among the poor, whatever you or your bank manager may feel about it, because you can read, which means that you are educated and literate, and therefore better able than most to cope with the world and "control" events. Even those of us who profess to be on the side of the poor will be asked by the biblical text, as we go back to it, in a memorable phrase that I read recently, "how can you talk poor and live rich?".

So my second slogan in this Forethought is "back to the text". If we can live by this slogan, we shall certainly be in for some uncomfortable surprises, but we shall also find ourselves drinking at an inexhaustible fountain.

Chapter 1

Is God at work

in this country today?

This book is being written in a particular country in a particular year. It is written in South Africa, at a time of quite momentous change, in the year of the first democratic elections in this country. We do not, as I write, yet know whether the elections will take place, and if they do how many of the political parties will take part. What we do know is that for all sections of the population immense changes are on the way, and naturally we respond to imminent changes with fear. Horrible things are going on, violence seems out of control, and unemployment is rising; many people ask "where can God possibly be in all this?" That is South Africa in 1994; but, as a matter of fact, I doubt if there is any place or any time when that question has not been asked with more or less anxiety or anger. I should like to take you to a moment of crisis in the history of Israel that seems in many ways very similar to this country and this time; and as you read about it, ask yourself whether it fits also the time and place in which you live. At the same time, ask yourself two questions: first, what are you at present afraid of, and, second, what signs would you point to that God is not working in this country at this moment? (And by "this country", I mean, of course, whatever country it is that you are reading and working in).

i) The end of everything: 587 BC

In the year 587, the history of Israel came to an end. King Zedekiah (aka Mattaniah) foolishly made a last attempt to rebel against Babylonian domination. Jerusalem was besieged for the second time in ten years; Zedekiah and his army fled but were captured. Then he was forced to see his sons murdered, and that was the last sight he saw, for his eyes were immediately put out, and he was led away in chains to exile in Babylon. The Temple was destroyed, the major houses in Jerusalem burnt to the ground, the walls of the city razed, and the population, or at any rate all those with leadership powers, led off into exile. You can read the grim tale in the last two chapters of the Second Book of Kings.

It seemed that it was the end of all that God had promised to Abraham, for example in Genesis 17:4-8, especially the promise that God "will give to you, and to your offspring after you, the land where you are now an alien, all the land of Canaan, for a perpetual holding; and I will be their God". They had lost the land, and some of them must have been wondering if they still had a God.

How did they react to this catastrophe? How would *you* react? We can detect in the books of the Old Testament five different responses to the exile, all of them familiar enough to us :

a) "there is no God"

This is not quite the atheist option that has become familiar enough in the Western world over the last two hundred years or so. It would be more a matter of deciding that the God that they had been worshipping all that time had turned out to be not particularly effective, so that it made more sense to worship another one, such as Bel or Marduk, Babylonian deities who had demonstrated their muscle-power by the destruction of Jerusalem. In the nature of things those who lost faith in God did not leave much trace in the pages of the Old Testament; but it may be at Jews who had taken this option that the remark in Isaiah 46:1-2 is aimed: "Bel bows, Nebo stoops, their idols are on beasts and cattle . . . they stoop, they bow down together; they cannot save the burden, but themselves go into captivity", along with all the polemic that you find against idols in Isaiah 40-55.

b) "wouldn't it be lovely to go home!"

This is the nostalgia of exiles, the helpless longing for return. It often comes accompanied with a certain unreality, an idealisation of the past and its beauties, as you can tell simply by eavesdropping on any gathering of those who are away from their country. Naturally, the Israelites in Babylon were also given to this sort of yearning for "the old country", and one of the most striking examples is in Psalm 137 (which is, incidentally, one of the few Psalms ever to have made it to the top of the charts) :

> *By the rivers of Babylon,*
> *there we sat down*
> *and there we wept*
> *when we remembered Zion.*

Or look at those chapters in the Isaiah scroll that were written during the years of exile, Isaiah 40-55, and just *feel* the longing in them.

c) "one Babylonian, one bullet"

This is a slightly altered version of a slogan that has been common enough in South Africa in recent years. Here the idea is that the oppressor is so evil that the only way to deal with him is to kill him. For an example of that you might look at those verses of Ps 137 that are never read out in church ("O daughter Babylon, you devastator, happy shall they be who pay you back what you have done to us! Happy shall they be who take your little ones and dash them against the rock!"), or at Isaiah 47:1-15, with its vindictive desire for Babylon to suffer.

d) "the lapse into dreaming"

Dreaming is one of the ways in which we cope with reality, and a prime example of a dreamer among those exiles in Babylon was Ezekiel, sitting there by the banks of the Chebar, and seeing visions of the chariots of God, and of God departing from Jerusalem, and of the reconstructed Temple, not to mention the Valley of the Dry Bones.

e) "get on with life and stop moaning"

Among all exiles you will also find this pragmatic option. The show, after all, must go on. A prime example of this would be the deep realism of the prophet Jeremiah, who in chapter 29 of his scroll writes a letter to the exiles that you would do well to read, telling them to "build houses and live in them, plant gardens and eat what they produce. Take wives and have sons and daughters; take wives for your sons, and give your daughters in marriage, that they may bear sons and daughters; multiply there, and do not decrease. But seek the welfare of the city where I have sent you into exile, and pray to the Lord on its behalf, for in its welfare you will find your welfare."

Which of these is the right reaction? In my view, all of them. You need, as the Bible does, to embrace a range of possible reactions to disaster, if you are to survive it; for different reactions are appropriate to different settings and to different people at different times. That may puzzle some readers : "how can the Bible countenance atheism?" they may ask, bristling with indignation. Well, atheism is no more than an invitation from God to purify our understanding of God. Read prayerfully through the book of Job, or through Qoheleth, for an example of profound questioning of conventional piety. And, likewise, though the exiles' nostalgia may be marked by elements of unreality, a pipedream is often an essential element for human beings in surviving a crisis. And even the option of taking up arms against evil is one that many sincere believers have embraced, both Jewish and Christian. We may not care for this option, but it is part of the range of human responses, and may be an authentic one. Similarly, Ezekiel's dreaming can help people to cope, and that is what God is always trying to do, to enable us to get through the present disaster into where God really wants us to be. Lastly, we shall never in fact survive catastrophe unless the defence mechanism switches on that enables us to "carry on", and Jeremiah's realism is also a necessary part of our response to God.

So you find in the Bible several different ways of coping with the ultimate catastrophe; but that should not blind us to the most remarkable fact of all, namely that Israel survived, and with its faith intact. Or rather, not intact, but profoundly purified. This really should not have happened, and to see why it did may help us to grasp the secret of reading the Bible today, out of whatever situation we find ourselves in. I should like to point to two features of Israel that enabled them to see God at work in their situation. And, of course, once we can see God at work then no situation is irremediable. The two features involve respectively looking *forward*, and looking *back*. They found themselves able to say, first, "our disaster was predicted all along", and, secondly, "there is hope for the future, but not in the way we expected". Let us take these two features separately, and, as we do so, ask "can we read the story of God's action in this country today?"

ii) The Predictions

The 8th century was a time of great prosperity in Israel, the more Northern of the two parts into which the kingdom had split after Solomon's reign. However, it seems that a prosperous society is not always in touch with its God, and this society, like many other societies that have become wealthy, had simply forgotten the demands of justice. Into this wealthy but decadent kingdom stalks a Southerner (never the most popular animal amongst Northerners), Amos of Tekoah, who does not pause to say "what a nice place you have here", or the other flattering things ordinarily expected of visitors, but lets them have it with both barrels. Imagine yourself to be a fairly well-to-do lady in the Northern suburbs of Mount Samaria, and how you might feel upon being addressed in these terms :

> *Hear this word, you cows of Bashan,*
> *who are on Mount Samaria*
> *who oppress the poor,*
> *who crush the needy,*
> *who say to their husbands:*
> *"Bring me something to drink" (4:1).*

This foreigner is not setting out to win friends and influence people, and there will be a good deal less enthusiasm for his message when they hear him say:

> *alas for those who lie on beds of ivory,*
> *and lounge on their couches*
> *and eat lambs from their flock, and calves from the stall;*
> *who sing idle songs to the sound of the harp . . .*
> *who drink wine from bowls*
> *and anoint themselves with the finest oils . . .*
> *Therefore they shall now be the first to go into exile,*
> *and the revelry of the loungers shall pass away (6:4-7).*

As far as Amos could see, indeed as far as the Bible can see, a society like that, built upon the disparity between rich and poor, simply cannot survive. We should do well to heed this warning ourselves; but instead, we are all too likely to try to shut it out, and, if the messenger gets too noisy, to shut him up. So the episode at Amos 7:10-15 should not surprise us, for when Amaziah priest of Bethel reports Amos to the king, and orders him to go home, he is only doing what the wealthy establishment will tend to do when faced with the subversive demands of justice. In reply, Amos simply asserts that this is his vocation; and that the establishment will have to pay for its deliberate deafness:

> *Therefore thus says the Lord:*
> *'Your wife shall become a prostitute in the city,*
> *and your sons and your daughters shall fall by the sword,*
> *and your land shall be parcelled out by line;*
> *you yourself shall die in an unclean land,*
> *and Israel shall surely go into exile away from its land' (7:17).*

The logic of an unjust society is that it will fall apart and die, rotten from within; and we cannot complacently sit back and gaze at biblical accounts of past societies that have died, for what was true then is true also now, and if our society is one marked by injustice and by a vast gap between rich and poor, then we should start asking ourselves where Amaziah is now.

Amos' slightly junior contemporary Hosea also stalks angrily through the Northern kingdom, saying the most horrendous things:

> *you have ploughed wickedness,*
> *you have reaped injustice,*
> *you have eaten the fruit of lies.*
> *Because you have trusted in your power*
> *and in the multitude of your warriors,*
> *therefore the tumult of war shall rise against your people,*
> *and all your fortresses shall be destroyed . . .*

Now the reason why these prophecies were preserved is simply that they came true. Few will have believed the belligerent and aggressive utterances of Amos and Hosea; but in 722 Samaria was captured by Assyria, and the

Israelites forcibly removed, never to be heard of again, while people from other parts of the Assyrian empire were settled in the Northern Kingdom, which kindled in the Southern Kingdom the deep suspicion of Samaritans and Galileans that lasted at least until the time of Jesus. You can read all about it in 2 Kings 17.

So Israel was deported, lost everything, and very little survived of the old confederacy, except that a few seem to have escaped to Judah, the Southern Kingdom, carrying with them the memory that Amos and Hosea had spoken the truth.

Not that the South was squeaky-clean. Some twenty years before the fall of Samaria, Isaiah heard the call of God, and like Amos he heard it in terms of the demands of justice. Few of his contemporaries in Jerusalem will have enjoyed being addressed as follows:

> *Hear the word of the Lord, you rulers of Sodom!*
> *Listen to the teaching of our God, you people of Gomorrah!*
> *(Isaiah 1:10),*

particularly when Isaiah went on to tell them that God disliked their sacrifices, burnt offerings, new moons, and even sabbaths and feast-days. It would be rather like a Catholic priest saying that going to mass is a waste of time.

For Isaiah it seemed self-evident that too much wealth cannot possibly be a good thing. Look, for example at 3:16-26, and especially these verses :

> *Because the daughters of Zion are haughty*
> *and walk with outstretched necks,*
> *glancing wantonly with their eyes,*
> *mincing along as they go, tinkling with their feet,*
> *the Lord will afflict with scabs the daughters of Zion*
> *and the Lord will lay bare their secret parts.*

It is hard to imagine anything more offensive than these lines, particularly if for Zion you substitute the name of the wealthiest suburb you know in this country. And many of the social evils that Isaiah denounces in God's name are familiar to us today, like the capacity of the rich to become ever richer:

> *You who join house to house, who add field to field*
> *until there is room for no one but you*
> *and you are left to live alone in the midst of the land ...*
> *You who rise early in the morning in pursuit of strong drink,*
> *who linger in the evening to be inflamed by wine ...*

It would be good to read the whole of Isaiah 5 from which these quotations are taken. And Isaiah is never afraid to attack the establishment when it is behaving unjustly (as establishments, I regret to say, instinctively tend to do):

> *You who make iniquitous decrees, who write oppressive statutes,*
> *to turn aside the needy for justice*
> *and to rob the poor of my people of their right,*
> *that widows may be your spoil*
> *and that you may make the orphans your prey,*
> *What will you do on the day of punishment?*

We need to shift uncomfortably in our seats as we hear this, and ask: "do these words apply to this country today?" For, like Amos, Isaiah could not see that a society operating in this way could possibly survive. Injustice, according to the Jewish and Christian tradition (though we have not always lived up to our tradition), is a deadly infection at the heart of a society, which in the end will destroy it from within. And, of course, what Isaiah said came true, which is a principal reason why his words have survived to this day.

Not that people seem to have listened very much to Isaiah; for a century or so later we find Jeremiah on the same tack. The message is the same, though the approach is rather different. One of the elements here is Jeremiah's idea of God's sadness at Judah's infidelity. Look for example at the astonishing things written in Jeremiah chapter 2, and the beginning of chapter 3, but do not read it in mixed company, for it is rather strong meat. In chapter 5 Jeremiah is actually driven to offer a challenge to his fellow-citizens, to come up with a single person acting justly in the whole of Jerusalem. And the chapter ends with the allegation that even the religious establishment are in cahoots with the unjust political establishment. Jeremiah cannot avoid the sense that doom is inevitably going to come as a result, and the reason is quite simple:

> *For from the least to the greatest of them,*
> *everyone is greedy for unjust gain;*
> *and from prophet to priest everyone deals falsely.*
> *They have treated the wound of my people carelessly,*
> *saying "Peace, Peace", when there is no peace (6:13).*

Now uttering this sort of stuff will win you few friends, particularly among the establishment, and we are not at all surprised when we read of the nasty little episode in chapter 36, when the king shows his contempt for the word of God by chopping bits off it and putting them in the fire that was burning to ward off the winter chill. Jehoiakim would have been well-advised to seek warmth of quite another kind. It was an easy matter for Jeremiah to dictate another scroll, even longer than the one that had experienced combustion; it would have been far more difficult, but far more urgent, for the ruling classes to root out injustice from Jerusalem.

And, once again, it all came true. In Jeremiah's lifetime, the Babylonians captured Jerusalem, and the exile started; a corrupt society ceased forever to exist, just as the various prophets had said it must, and the remainder went off to settle by the River Chebar and muse over what had gone wrong, and how they could possibly cope with the disaster. Jerusalem was utterly sacked, and if you want to know what things were like in that city at that time, just read the Book of Lamentations, which follows Jeremiah in the Bible. It is sometimes supposed to have been written by Jeremiah, though it was not; but the five poems that make it up certainly describe the mood in the sacked city after 587.

iii) The Hope for the Future

So it had all been predicted, and it happened. However, simply being able to say "I told you so" does not of itself provide hope for the future. It is a beginning, however, for if you can correctly argue that a society built on injustice cannot survive, because that runs counter to God's intentions, then the collapse of such a society is a sign of the working of God, and unless God is some kind of megalomaniac tyrant, bent on blind cruelty (an option that for the most part the Jews were not prepared to consider), then there is some hope, for God must be always working for good, to enhance life rather than destroy it.

Already in Hosea there are signs of hope emerging; there is nothing of the sort in Amos, or those parts of the Amos scroll that the prophet actually wrote, but Hosea is a different matter. He does see hope, not because he is particularly inclined to suppose that the humans to whom he addresses himself are at all likely to mend their ways, but simply because God is God. So there is a beautiful passage at 11:1, describing God's relationship to Israel, in terms of a loving mother:

> When Israel was a child, I loved him,
> and out of Egypt I called my son.
> The more I called them, the more they went from me . . .
> Yet it was I who taught Ephraim to walk,
> I took them up in my arms, but they did not know that I healed them.
> I led them with cords of human kindness, with bands of love,
> I was to them like those who lift infants to their cheeks.
> I bent down to them and fed them (Hosea 11:1-4).

We do not need to be told that a God who can use this passionately intimate language is not suddenly going to turn round and reject Israel utterly.

So it is that even in Jeremiah, in the so-called "Book of Consolation", there are signs of hope, which are all the more striking for one who was so constitutionally gloomy a prophet. You could do worse than go through chapters 30-33, looking for indications that all will turn out well, and making a list of them. In particular you will notice the following lines from chapter 31:

> See, I am going to bring them from the land of the north,
> and gather them from the farthest parts of the earth,
> among them the blind and the lame,
> those with child and those in labour, together
> a great company, they shall return here.
> With weeping they shall come,
> and with consolations I shall lead them back (8-9).

And there are plenty of other such lines in the chapter, but read and relish verse 20, for its tender warmth:

> Is Ephraim my dear son? Is he the child I delight in?
> As often as I speak against him, I still remember him.
> Therefore I am deeply moved for him; I will surely have mercy on him.

And compare the remarkable promise of a new covenant in verses 31-34. The point of all this is that God still loves passionately even those who have built an unjust society. There is hope here for all of us.

The dreamer Ezekiel, too, offers hope to the exiles. He teaches them that God can appear even by the waters of Babylon, for the prophet was "among the exiles by the River Chebar" (1:1) when he saw his first visions of God. He gave them also an audacious dream, of God leaving the Temple in Jerusalem, and travelling Eastwards, clearly towards Babylon and the bewildered exiles (10:18-19). Ezekiel also makes another important contribution, for he counters the fears of those who recognise that a previous generation had done evil, and were alarmed that they might be punished for what their parents had done. It is a splendid treatment of the subject that he offers in chapter 18, and you would do well to sit down and read it through slowly. What Ezekiel is doing here is to insist on the doctrine of personal responsibility, not as opposed to corporate responsibility (i.e. our part in the structural injustices of our society), but in contrast to the idea that a blindly retributive God might punish us for what we have not done. And, best of all, in the second half of the chapter, Ezekiel teaches that it is always possible to change the direction of our lives: the wicked can always repent (of course, by the same token, it is equally possible for the righteous to start doing wicked things), and that is the invitation to all of us from Ezekiel's God. In order to repent, however, Israel has to realise that it has sinned, so Ezekiel tells a fairly crude parable, contrasting the love of God and the ingratitude of those on whom God's love has been lavished. You must read chapter 16 on your own, and you will see why it is not ordinarily read out in church;

but more important, try to see what the parable is saying. And when you have done that, go on to chapter 23 for another dose of fairly strong stuff. I think that you will agree that you would be surprised to hear it proclaimed as a text, still less preached on, next Sunday.

And, most importantly of all, Ezekiel insists that the exiles must not lose hope, that they must allow God to be God. That is what the splendid vision of the Valley of the Dry Bones ("Dem bones, dem bones, dem dry bones, now hear the Word of the Lord") in chapter 37:1-14 is all about. And the long, and it must be confessed, not all that enthralling, vision of the New Temple, in chapters 40-48, is likewise a dramatic exhortation not to lose hope.

In a quite different way, the historians of Israel who wrote at this time were also finding signs of hope. Writing history at all is of course a sign of hope, for you do not write about the past unless you suspect that it may enable you to steer a course through the uncertain future. In particular, there were those historians who wrote, or, more accurately, revised, the history of Israel from the moment they entered the Promised Land, through the conquest, and that penumbral intervening period which we call (because we do not know what else to call it) the time of the Judges, to the Israelites' invention of the monarchy, and the sad story of the inner decay of the two kingdoms until they were carried off into exile. This is the continuous history that is covered in the Books of Joshua, Judges, 1 and 2 Samuel, and the 1st and 2nd Books of Kings; to it was added, as a kind of programmatic preface, to remind Israel what kind of a community it ought to be if it was to survive, the Book of Deuteronomy. The historian or historians who compiled this book were not doing quite what a modern historian would seek to do, for the methods of scientific historiography were quite unknown to them; but it was certainly something similar, for they were asking the question: how did we get where we are today? And to do this, they used old archival material from the monarchy, and folk-tales handed down in the religious shrines, and various other sources as well. It seems that there were two editions of this history, one before the monarchy fell, and one after the disaster had happened, as the dazed survivors licked their wounds and wondered where God was in all this. And the conclusion they came to was that prayerful reflection on the events since the heady days of the Conquest when all (in retrospect at any rate) seemed blissfully easy, revealed a pattern in Israel's history. The pattern they detected was as follows: God's generous gift was always followed by Israel's infidelity; then came in succession the inevitable punishment, Israel's repentance, and eventual restoration. So there was hope even in this major catastrophe; if Israel would repent, then restoration must be just round the corner, and God was after all at work in the people's history.

Another group that was examining Israel's traditions at this time, and seeking to find hope in them, was the Priests. They looked, not at the history of the land from the time Israel entered it to the time they left it, as the Deuteronomic Historians had done, but at its early history, though the word history is used only loosely here. The Priests had of course no job, now that the Temple had been destroyed; but they still had the traditions, and they meditated on these, to work out what had happened, and how disaster might be avoided in future. They actually seem to have recast a good many of the earliest traditions of Israel, and to have provided a narrative framework on which to hang these traditions. Such a powerful impact did they have on the text of the Old Testament that scholars actually refer to P, or the "Priestly Writer", and if you want a rapid introduction to the kind of things that interest "P", then you might look at the first chapter of Genesis, or the last chapter of Exodus. Genesis 1 gives an account of Creation that is completely different from what you find in chapter 2; and it is much later than that version of our origins. In chapter 1 you will find the Priestly Writer's obsession with order, and separation of conflicting elements, and feasts, and the sabbath; the very division of creation into seven days reflects Priestly interests. As it happens, it is rather artificially done, as you can see from the fact that on days 3 and 6 God has to work twice as hard as on other days, in order to get everything created. And for another insight into the Priestly writer's mentality, look at what he (or they) has done with the Exodus story, especially the bits that are not normally read out in church. The book starts with the splendidly racy account of Moses childhood, and young manhood, and his escape to Midian, after having had the misfortune to kill an Egyptian; and the story goes rapidly through Moses' call, his battles with Pharaoh, the plagues, the Passover, the crossing of the Red Sea, the first account of the gift of manna, and the water from the rock. But from chapter 19 onwards the book becomes, rather unexpectedly, a code of laws. And chapter 25 to 31 is a description of how the tabernacle and its accoutrements are to look. This description is separated from the last chapters of the book by a return to the racier style in the account of the Golden Calf and its aftermath. Then in 35-40 the tabernacle that has been described is now built, in language virtually identical to chapters 25-31. The Priestly writer has really imposed his (or one should say "their") interests on what was originally a simple story of liberation. In this context the way in which P has ended the book of Exodus is very striking. Read 40:34-38, where the Priests saw Israel operating as it should operate, with God in the tabernacle guiding the people on their journey, and the people obediently responsive.

And if you are shifting restlessly and asking what all these descriptions of priestly vestments have to do with Israel's surviving the catastrophe of exile, the answer, for the Priestly Writer, is that the people is to find hope by gathering in obedience round the tabernacle of its God, worshipping God in the divinely appointed way, and waiting humbly for God to give the word.

Lastly, Israel found hope for the future in the remarkable work of the anonymous poet-prophet whose writings got attached to the Isaiah scroll, chapters 40-55, whom we call Second (or Deutero-) Isaiah. This person is certainly not identical with First Isaiah, who prophesied in Jerusalem in the 8th century, but he may have been part of the Isaiah school, inheriting the traditions of Isaiah ben Amoz. He found hope, not in examining the past, but in meditating on God's creative and recreative powers. He also read his newspaper, for he knew about the young lion Cyrus who was on the rise at this point (the 40's of the 6th century BCE), and had the audacity to call him "God's Messiah" (45:1) "though you do not know me". In the vigorous new political change that Cyrus represented, our prophet saw God working for the restoration of Judah, and the return home of the exiles. He meditated on two key elements of Israel's prehistory, the Creation and the Exodus, and presented the return home as a new creation and a new exodus that would far outweigh anything that had hitherto happened to the people. His slogan was "you ain't seen nothing yet". This daring theology enabled him to tell the people that God was going to take them home, and that the last state would be a good deal better than the first. He also meditated on the grim things that can sometimes happen to faithful disciples of the Lord, and produced what we know as the four "Songs of the Suffering Servant", which the Church uses as part of the Holy Week liturgy; but that is another matter. For our purposes, the essential thing about him is that in his very creative and original way he gave his people hope when there seemed to be no hope.

iv) Conclusions

The conclusions of this chapter, if you have managed to follow all the way through, are fairly obvious, and they are what we said at the beginning; but they are worth restating, along with the challenging question: do they apply to our society today?

The first conclusion is: *you have been warned* - a society founded on injustice cannot survive, and you must expect punishment if your society is like that.

The second is: *it is never too late to repent.* God never withdraws the divine love, is always seeking to nurture our human existence and make it grow, and it is always possible for us to turn back to that love.

Chapter 2

How A Biblical Story Works

(Mk 10:17-31)

In this chapter, I should like to do with you something you can really do for yourself, namely to read a biblical story and try and see what it is doing to us, for gospel is not gospel until it is having its effect on our lives. The story I have chosen is the account in Mark's gospel of the meeting between Jesus and the rich man, and I shall do nothing with this story that you could not do, if you read it often enough and attentively enough.

The story is to be found in chapter 10 of Mark's gospel, which in many ways is the weightiest chapter in Mark. It may be helpful to set it in its wider context (and it would really help if you had the bible open at this point); we can start by going back to 9:31, where we learn that Jesus is instructing his disciples about the kind of Messiah that they are following, one who is journeying towards Jerusalem and the passion: "the Son of Man is being handed over into human hands, and they will kill him, and having been killed after three days he will rise up". Not surprisingly, we are told that the disciples "had no idea about this remark, and they were afraid to ask"(9:32). All the way through this gospel, Mark is attempting to answer two questions: first, "who is this Jesus?" and, second, "what must his disciples be like?" Again and again the two questions are seen to belong together, and here we can see the connection between the Son of Man's journey to death and the disciples' blank incomprehension.

In its more immediate context (and with Scripture it is always essential to look at the context), it is preceded in chapter 10 by the encounter with some "little children" (10:13-16), and followed by a disquisition on discipleship and "leaving all" (10:23-31), and then by Jesus' third prediction of his passion (for the other two, look at 8:31 and 9:31, and see how immediately after these predictions you get a blunder by one or more disciples). And then comes the absurd request of James and John (10: 35-45). These two silly boys, who were among the first disciples that Jesus called, have obviously not listened to a word that he has been saying, when they ask for a blank cheque: "Teacher, we want you to do for us whatever we ask you", and it turns out that what they are after is the top places in the new dispensation: "to sit one on your right and one on the left in your glory".

So the whole context of this story, which is one you know very well, is about discipleship, and about disciples who don't really understand what following Jesus is all about. That should make a difference to the way in which we read the story of the rich man (by the way, notice that he is here not a rich *young* man; and you might just look in your copy of the New Testament and see which gospel it is that presents him as a young man). What I am going to do is simply to read the story with you, using my own translation. You can check it against the text in your Bible.

This is how it goes :

> And as he was going onto the road,
> running up ONE and genuflecting to him interrogated him,
>
> Good teacher, what shall I do that I may inherit eternal life?
> But Jesus said to him, why do you call me good?
>
> No one is good except ONE, God.
>
> You know the commandments: do not kill,
> do not commit adultery,
> do not steal,
> do not bear false witness,
> do not deprive,
> honour your father and mother.
>
> But he said to him: Teacher, all these things I have kept
> from my youth.
> But Jesus looking at him loved him and said to him:
> one thing you lack:
> go, what you have, sell and give to the poor
> and you will have treasure in heaven,
> and come, follow me
> but he became gloomy at the word and went away grieving,
> for he was having many possessions.

See, firstly, how the story starts: Jesus is described as "going onto the road". In other words, he is "approaching" it; normally in this gospel he is "on the road", which for Mark's readers is the road of discipleship. (See, for example, 2:23, 6:8, 8:27; 9:33-34, 10:32,46,52; 11:8; 12:14). So Mark is telling us that the incident which is about to take place has to do with someone (or some people, for we have not reached the story yet) who is not really yet on the way of discipleship.

Next comes this odd sentence: "running up ONE and genuflecting to him interrogated him". There are a number of things to be said about this. In the first place, we are surely meant to be struck by the man's boyish enthusiasm. Secondly, though, there is an oddity in the way he is described : not, as we should expect in Greek, "a certain one", but ONE. A Jewish reader of Mark's gospel would inevitably have thought about the God whom they proclaim each day to be ONE. Thirdly, we cannot help feeling that by running up and genuflecting in this way, the man is rather taking the short cut to discerning who Jesus is. In contrast to this slightly extravagant, and perhaps rather presumptuous, gesture, see 7:24 ("he did not want anyone to know"), where Jesus, as elsewhere in the gospel, is very cautious about revealing who he is. It is worth noting that in Mark's gospel only one other person does this action of genuflecting to Jesus, namely the leper at 1:40, but that is not in all the manuscripts. So there is already a feeling in the reader that the man is rushing it, trying to take a short cut to something that we can only learn painfully slowly. And, in case we had not picked up all these other clues, Mark actually tells us that the man "interrogated" Jesus. This is no way for a prospective disciple to behave.

Fourthly, we notice that the man here takes the initiative. This happens on two other occasions in Mark, first when Jesus' mother and brothers at 3:31 "standing outside sent to him and summoned him", and second when the former demoniac in the country of the Gerasenes at 5:18 asks "that he might be with him"; and both groups get rebuked for it. In this gospel, it is normally Jesus who takes the initiative. So at 1:17 and 20 it is Jesus who summons the two sets of brothers; at 2:14 Levi of Alphaeus is ordered to follow Jesus; and at 3:13, before appointing the twelve, Jesus "called those he wanted". Discipleship is not something that we opt for, but something that is given us. So we are already clear that this man is out of order.

Next, the man addresses Jesus as "good teacher". Now elsewhere in the gospel (and I'll let you find the references) "teacher" is the correct way of addressing Jesus. But "good teacher" is found nowhere else; and indeed, the only other use of the word "good" is at 3:14, in a debate about healing on the Sabbath. So this deepens our sense that the man is getting it wrong here.

Lastly, Mark tells us what was the man's request. It is something that we do not come across anywhere else in the gospel: "what shall I do in order to inherit eternal life?" Mark does not really talk about what Jesus has to offer in terms of "eternal life", except at 10:30; and theword "inherit", which suggests a kind of *right* to eternal life, appears nowhere else in the gospel.

Now at this point the reader may be getting impatient, noticing that we are still only on the first verse of the story after all this time. Well, I shan't spend as long as this on the other verses, you will be glad to know. But see how the story draws us in. Just by pausing to look closely at a tiny part of a story that every Bible-reader knows well, we have been able to pick up a good deal about the mood of the story, and make it our own. This is something that you should be doing for yourself with every biblical story you read, to make it come alive in this country, today.

And, before going on to the next verses, it is worth asking: what is *our* question to Jesus? Are we, like this man, inclined to ask for the easy way in? Or what is the question that we put to the Lord as a country today? Are we prepared to follow on the way of a costly discipleship or not? That is the challenge that Mark puts before us.

In the next verse, we are given Jesus' response:

> But Jesus said to him, why do you call me good?
> No one is good except ONE, God.

It must be said that this is abrupt and inconsequential, and perhaps reminds us of Jesus' response to the Syrophoenician woman in 7:27. But at least she got what she was looking for! This man, having interrogated Jesus, is now interrogated in return, and asked why he uses the apparently unexceptionable adjective "good". Then Jesus goes on with the lesson: "none is good but ONE: God", and we are reminded of the remark at 2:7, when Jesus has said to the paralytic "your sins are forgiven", and some scribes mutter "blasphemy - who can forgive sins, but ONE: God", to which Mark may want us to reply "exactly". For similar examples of questions that leap of the page of the gospel, and point to the mystery of who Jesus is, see 4:41 and 8:29. Mark may want us to see the ONE who ran up as getting the roles wrong, playing at God (the only ONE worthy of the title, as any Jew would know) and doing what in fact only Jesus can do.

Having made this point, Jesus goes on to give a rather conventional list of commandments to obey:

> You know the commandments:
> do not kill,
> do not commit adultery,
> do not steal,
> do not bear false witness,
> do not deprive,
> honour your father and mother.

And we nod wisely at this list; but if we reflect for a second, we also note a rather casual air in what Jesus says. For one thing, these commandments are not in the right order (check it and see if you don't believe me); for another thing Jesus adds "do not deprive", which is a new commandment, possibly one which we are supposed to imagine as particularly suitable to the man's spiritual life. For another thing, there is a very remarkable omis-

sion. There is nothing here of the immensely solemn material in Exodus
20:1-11, all that material about what God has done for the People of God,
and how they must behave towards God. Many scholars suggest that what
Jesus is doing is to emphasise the importance for this man of correct moral
relations with other human beings, something that in his blithe arrogance he
had not yet realised. And at this stage we feel that the interview is not going
at all well. But we have noticed only this because we took time to see what
Mark wrote, not what we think he must have written. And you can see, I
hope, that I am not inventing this: it is all there in the text.

Then in the next verse comes what I can only describe as a piece of
breathtaking insouciance, the man more or less saying: "teacher . . . I have
nothing to learn":

> But he said to him: Teacher,
> all these things I have kept
> from my youth.

We are bound to feel uneasy at the idea of someone claiming to have
observed all the commandments since he was a child. Hands up the reader
of this book who makes such a claim without blushing. But even if it is true
what the man says here, he is not really listening to the answer Jesus gives
to his question.

Then comes really quite an astonishing verse:

> But Jesus looking at him loved him and said to him:
> one thing you lack:
> go, what you have, sell and give to the poor
> and you will have treasure in heaven,
> and come, follow me

First of all, it says that Jesus "looked at" the man. There are only two
other occasions in the whole of Mark's gospel when this word is used, at
10:27, when Jesus "looks at" the disciples puzzling over the question of
who can be saved; and 14:67, where it is the maidservant, "looking at"
Peter before accusing him of being a member of Jesus' group. So each time
that we hear the word the context is that of the difficulties of discipleship.

Secondly, the evangelist says that Jesus "loved" the man. Now this verb
is nowhere else used in Mark except when the evangelist is citing the Old
Testament. So if we have been reading the gospel carefully we are really
sitting up and listening. And only now does the man receive an invitation:
"come, follow me", which in this gospel is the standard invitation to discipleship. We remember how on every other occasion that someone was invited to discipleship, at 1:17, 20 (the two sets of brothers), at 2:14 (Levi of
Alphaeus), and 3:13 (the twelve) it was at *Jesus'* initiative. In this story, it is

the man who takes the initiative; eventually he is granted the same invitation that was given to the two sets of brothers and to Levi of Alphaeus; but already we are aware that the interview has not gone as it might be expected to have gone.

And so it turns out in the next verse:

> *but he became gloomy at the word and went away grieving,*
> *for he was having many possessions.*

So the story ends, as it began, with the man getting discipleship wrong. He started by asking about how he could purchase eternal life, and now he ends by grieving, because he cannot manage to respond to the invitation. The word that I have translated as "grieving" appears again at 14:19 in this gospel, where it describes how the disciples reacted to Jesus' prediction that one of them was to betray him. In our story, which is a very sad story, the grief comes because, unlike the two sets of brothers who left everything and followed Jesus, this man cannot pay the price implied by that blithe request of his with which the story began. For a similar story in the Old Testament, see the tale of Elisha and the Shunamitess in 1Kings 4, and see how the woman there wants to take the initiative at verses 10 and 16; by the end, however, at verses 36 and 37, she is thoroughly chastened by her experience, and at last prepared to leave the prophet wholly in charge.

So there is a great deal in this story, if we will only read it carefully and let it work its magic on us, if we can accept its invitation to "step aboard" and become part of the story. And, obviously, it has much to say to us who live in this country today about what it means to be a disciple of Jesus.

The Marcan Sandwich

We have not, however, yet grasped the full meaning of the story. In Mark's gospel (well, actually, in all of Scripture, but it is Mark that we are looking at just for the moment), you always have to look at the context, as we have said. And Mark has a knack of "sandwiching" stories, wrapping them round each other, and encouraging us to interpret the one story by the other. There are many examples of this in this gospel; but if you want to look at two good ones, try the two women whose stories are intertwined in 5:21-43, or the extraordinary stories of the cursing of the fig tree and the cleansing of the Temple which shed light on each other in chapter 11 (12-22).

So it is here, for Mark has framed this story of the rich man with two other stories that help us to understand it.

The first of these is the beautiful story in verses 13-16:

> *And they were bringing to him children,*
> *that he might touch them.*

> *But the disciples upbraided them.*

> *But seeing it Jesus was angry and he said to them:*
> *allow the little children to come to me, do not stop them,*
> *for of such is the Reign of God.*

> *Amen I say to you, whoever does not receive*
> *the Reign of God like a little child*
> *will no way enter into it.*

> *And taking them in his arms*
> *he blessed them, laying his hands upon them.*

Notice that it starts, "and they were bringing to him little children", and we remember perhaps the four who brought the paralytic in 2:3, where the same verb is used. In both cases, the children and the paralytic come to Jesus, not on their own initiative, but because others have brought them, whereas the rich man sought Jesus out, and asked a rather condescending question of him.

Here the disciples react; Mark says of them that they "upbraided". Now this is something of a battle-word in Mark's gospel. So we read that Jesus on several occasions "upbraids" a spirit (1:25; 3:12; 9:25). Jesus also "upbraids" the wind and the disciples (4:39; 8:30). Very daringly, Mark has Peter "upbraid" Jesus at 8:32, a key moment in the unfolding of the gospel, and in the very next verse neatly turns the tables, using the same verb. Finally, the crowds "upbraid" Bartimaeus at 10:48, because they think he has the wrong attitude to Jesus. But the crowds are wrong there, and the disciples are wrong here, as we now discover when Mark tells us of Jesus' reaction: "he was angry", as those same dim-witted disciples will be "angry" with James and John in 10:41, proving that they have understood not a word of all that Jesus has been trying to teach them about discipleship. And Jesus' verdict is the devastating one, incomprehensible to those adult disciples, whose reactions were far too adult for their own good:

> *of such is the reign of God.*

And this story ends with one of the most beautiful of all the gestures attributed to Jesus in the gospel:

> *And taking them in his arms he blessed them, laying his hands upon them,*

having previously made the extraordinary statement:

> *Amen I say to you, whoever does not receive*
> *the Reign of God like a little child*
> *will no way enter into it,*

which we now see was precisely what the rich man had failed to grasp. That, then is the first bit of the "sandwich". Now let us look at what comes after our story. It takes the form of some reflecting out loud on the scene that has just taken place:

> And looking round Jesus says to his disciples:
> How with difficulty those who have things will enter
> into the Reign of God!
>
> But the disciples were dumbstruck at his words
> and Jesus responded to them again:
> Children, how difficult it is to enter into the Reign of God!
>
> It is easier for a camel to go through a needle-eye
> than for a rich person to enter the Reign of God.
>
> But they were very very amazed, saying to themselves:
> And who can be saved?
>
> Looking at them Jesus says:
> for humans it is impossible, but not for God,
> since all things are possible for God.
>
> Peter began to say to him:
> see, we have left all things and have followed you . . .
>
> Jesus said: Amen I say to you,
> there is no one who has left
> house or brothers or sisters or mother or father or children or fields
> for my sake and for the sake of the gospel,
> who does not receive a hundredfold now in this time
> houses and brothers and sisters and mothers and children and fields
> with persecutions,
> and in the age to come age-long life.
>
> But many first will be last and last first.

Once again we find reference to "entering the reign of God". The children were able to do that, but the rich man was not. Mark then reveals to us the disciples' reaction: they were "dumbstruck", as they will be again (though it is a different word that is used), in a few verses time at 10:32. Once again we have the sense that discipleship is something impossibly difficult to grasp.

Then Jesus offers an expansion of his teaching. Significantly, he addresses them as "children", making us think of the first part of the "sandwich", and repeating (though if you look closely it is not quite a repetition, is it?), how difficult it is to enter the reign of God. Then comes the famous saying about the camel and the needle's eye; and the point of the saying is simply that it is very difficult to enter the Kingdom of Heaven if you are rich; but see the squirming that some Scripture scholars go through to avoid facing this conclusion. We are meant to squirm, and then to accept the truth, that this gospel is to be read "from below", with the eyes of the poor, which is something that our rich man, taking the initiative with Jesus, had signally failed to do.

Once again we are given a reaction: "the disciples were very very amazed". Mark here underlines, not so much, I think the stupidity of the disciples, as the difficulty of the message. For we have always to remember that the gospel is our story, and these disciples whom we watch scratching their befuddled heads are you and I, as we ask "then who can be saved?"

We are not however left for long in our difficulty, for the evangelist provides a resolution, the only possible one in the circumstances: and it starts, as we saw earlier, with Jesus looking at them, and ends with the verdict: "for humans it is impossible, but not for God, for everything is possible for God". Then Peter asks the question that trembles on the lips of all would-be disciples, fearful that we may have made a dreadful mistake:

> *Peter began to say to him:*
> *see, we have left all things and have followed you.*

Now we know this to be true from what we have already seen when Peter was first called, when Mark tells us quite simply that "straightaway leaving their nets they followed him" (1:18); two verses later James and his brother John do the same thing: "and leaving their father Zebedee in the boat with the hired men they went after him"; and Matthew of course does the same at 2:14: "and rising up he followed him". So it is both a perfectly good question, and in fact a description of what Mark expects disciples to have done.

We wait therefore with a good deal of attentiveness for Jesus' answer, which is the longest speech he has made in this episode:

> *Jesus said: Amen I say to you,*
> *there is no one who has left*
> *house or brothers or sisters or mother or father or children or fields*
> *for my sake and for the sake of the gospel,*
>
> *who does not receive a hundredfold now in this time*
> *houses and brothers and sisters and mothers and children and fields*
> *with persecutions,*
> *and in the age to come age-long life.*
>
> *But many first will be last and last first.*

Discipleship for Mark is an extraordinarily radical business, we are learning. It is not something that you choose for yourself, but something to which you are invited. It demands nothing less than everything, and has nothing to do with the way the world sees things. Zebedee, left stunned in his boat with the hired servants, will not have found much consolation in the idea that the first are to be last and *vice versa*. In our story, which we have seen to be a very full one, the rich man was not a particularly good disciple; in fact he was not a disciple at all. The real heroes were the children, very definitely last on most people's lists, but singled out by Jesus for that exceptionally special gesture that showed that they were really first, of taking them in his arms and blessing them.

Jesus' values are such as to disconcert and challenge us, and in the next chapter we shall see how two of the evangelists described his birth and infancy, and how those stories challenge our comfortable preconceptions. In the following chapter we shall look at the Beatitudes, where Jesus explicitly lays his values before all would-be disciples.

Chapter 3

The Irrelevance of the

Well-to-Do

In the first chapter, we looked at ways in which Israel sought for signs that God was working in their world, after the catastrophe of the exile, and we saw that their prayerful reflection on that disaster led them, in various different ways, to ask themselves about the values on which they were operating, and the contrast of those values with the values of God. The second chapter looked at a particular story, Mark's account of the rich man who approached Jesus asking how to inherit eternal life, which turned out to be an acted parable of discipleship and pseudo-discipleship. In this third chapter I should like to look with you at the Christmas stories in the gospels of Matthew and Luke, to see what they tell us of the values that discipleship imposes on us. Who are the people that God is most interested in?

Christmas can be awful wherever it is celebrated. You feel in duty bound to "have a good time", as family members come back from far distant places. Often, however, their return upsets the finely balanced dynamics at home, and the problem is frequently exacerbated by drink, and by the fact that we all feel that it "ought not to be like this". In South Africa we have all these problems, made much worse by the peculiar conditions that obtain here. In the Zulu parish that I know best, for example, we do not have midnight mass, because it is dangerous for black people to be out at night.

And things get worse when we open the Bible, and are captivated by the warmth of the Infancy Narratives, especially in Luke's version. Then we remember the Christmas joys of childhood (or what we now imagine them to have been), and we wonder what went wrong. I should like to suggest that what is wrong is simply that we read those stories in the wrong way. We think of Christmas as a feast of the well-to-do, and of those who can afford to celebrate with large quantities of food and drink. Therefore if Christmas is not going well, the only thing to do is to open another bottle, slaughter another turkey, or buy even more expensive presents. But, as Charles

Dickens spotted 150 years ago, that is not the answer to the problem of Christmas.

For it is my contention that the Infancy narratives celebrate in rather daring ways the importance of the marginalised, and of those who could not possibly afford to celebrate the feast in the way that the advertisements put before us. The Infancy Narratives cry out to be read, that is to say, "from below", through the eyes of the poor and the oppressed. Only then is it possible to experience their warmth in our own lives.

i) *Matthew's stories of Jesus' birth*

a) Mt 1:1-17 "The Most Boring Bit of the NT"

This is already clear in the first of the stories, the opening of Matthew's gospel. In the Catholic Church, it is given as the gospel for December 17th, and many is the priest who has pretended that he thought the date was the 16th or 18th, in order to avoid having to preach on this text. But if we can only read it as Matthew's first readers would have taken it, we shall not find it such an obstacle. For Matthew sets out Jewish history in a highly stylised form, dividing it into three groups of fourteen generations each, from Abraham, to whom the original promise was given, to David, in whom the promise appeared, deceptively, to be fulfilled; then to the Exile, where the promise meets catastrophic failure, and, finally, the *real* fulfilment in Jesus. This neat mathematical arrangement is not intended to make us gasp with astonishment at an extraordinary genealogical coincidence. What Matthew's readers would have seen immediately is that seven is the number of perfection (and don't ask what "twice perfection" means!); and they will have grasped the coded message, which is simply that God's purposes never work out in quite the way we expect; but they do work out.

In addition, as many scholars have noted, four women are mentioned in the first eleven verses. Matthew's readers will have pricked up an alert ear at this, and they will not have needed to reach for their Bibles to be told that all of them were, or might have been foreigners, and all of them were associated with some kind of sexual irregularity, Tamar who pretended to be a prostitute, Rahab who actually was a member of that ancient profession, Ruth who climbed into bed with Boaz and became David's great-grandmother, and of course Mrs Uriah, who was the mother of Solomon. God uses the last people in the world you would expect, and God's purposes go ahead through and despite and because of the things that we humans do. That is a message that many people need to hear in this country today.

b) Mt 2:1-12 The Powerful Up to No Good

The same inversion of our ordinary human priorities is evident in my next passage. Matthew starts with a mention of Jesus, then places the reader in familiar Old Testament territory, Bethlehem of Judaea, and we feel comfortable. Then, however, he causes a chill to run down the spine, with the mention of Herod. For Matthew's Jewish readers knew perfectly well that virtually any member of that family was mad and bad, and up to no good whatever. Then he introduces, as independent witnesses, some characters whom he describes as *magoi,* which could be astrologers, magicians, or charlatans. But it seems that they are introduced in the guise of "independent experts" for we discover in verse 2 that they are correct in the conclusions that they have drawn from their star-gazing.

Correct they may be; but they are also so politically naive that they ask a decidedly tactless question: "where is the one born King of the Jews?" And we notice that this is the second mention of the word "king" in as many verses. We learn now that they want to worship, and this in Matthew's gospel is a *correct* reaction to the presence of Jesus (see 4:9, 8:2, 9:18, 14:33 15:35, 20:20, 28:9,17 for other examples of it). Then comes a splendid comment from the evangelist: "hearing this, Herod was disturbed, and all Jerusalem with him", and we can hear the foundations of the city, and of Herod's monarchy, quaking at the revelation. Whoever is right here, it is clearly not the powerful or the well-do-do. Then verse 4 makes it clear that Herod believes that the Magi are correct, and that it is possible to know where the Messiah is to be born. In this verse, it is possible to feel that Matthew is almost overplaying his hand, for he describes Herod as "synagoguing" all the religious establishment. That, at any rate, is what the Greek word says, though it is customarily translated as "gathering together". Matthew's point is clear: the religious establishment knows the truth about Jesus, and collaborates with the interests of the powerful, for whom the birth of Christ is "bad news", in attempting to eliminate the threat posed by this child. So they compliantly consult their works of reference in verses 5 and 6, and come up with "Bethlehem" as the correct answer.

Now Matthew presents us with Herod, the most powerful person we have seen so far in the gospel, as the archetypal villain. For Matthew's readers, the mere mention of his name will have led them to expect skulduggery, but the deft addition of the adverb "secretly" colours the whole of the rest of the verse; like the Jesuits beloved of a certain kind of British fiction, he is bound to be doing something sinister. And it becomes more sinister yet, when we learn that Herod "enquired carefully", for this tells us that he knows that it is true, what these *magoi* say, that the child is to be born as a king, and in Bethlehem. So it is with a growing sense of horror that we hear Herod speak of the "dear little child". Then once again we hear talk of "worship": "so that I too may come and worship him", but we fear that Herod's understanding of worship may not bode well for the child; so we are left nervously wondering how it will all turn out, but confident that God is in charge.

Finally, in verse 9, our independent experts get there; they find the "dear little child", and exhibit the correct reaction to him, namely "joy". Then for the first time in the gospel we see what appropriate "worship" might be, as they give gifts, of gold, frankincense, and myrrh, which symbolically represent the child as King, Priest and Suffering Redeemer.

And, at last, in verse 12, God effortlessly foils Herod, and we stand on our seats and applaud as the *magoi* are diverted back to their own place. And with the experts, the theme of kingship also disappears until the end of the gospel, where it reappears with a certain ambiguity (look at the following texts: 21:5; 27:11,29,37,42, and as you do so, ask: is he or is he not a king? What does it mean to be a king?) At all events, this baby is not a king in the normal sense, and God does not operate in the way we should normally expect, and certainly not in the interests of the powerful.

c) Mt 2:13-23 The powerless protected by God

This is the end of Matthew's infancy story, and startling things now happen; but because of what we have already seen we are confident all the time that the result will not be disastrous. The child becomes a refugee, in Egypt of all places (and as we read this, we should be jumping from our chairs in astonishment, for Egypt is the "old enemy"). It comes, of course, as no surprise to learn that Herod is proposing to kill the child; we knew all along that this would be the kind of "worship" that he had in mind. We note in passing that the journey is to be undertaken at night, and reflect that travelling at night is what refugees do, so that once again Matthew presents Jesus as firmly in solidarity with the dispossessed. And also, of course, Matthew presents the whole episode as a kind of reverse Exodus, as the hope of Israel is forced to take refuge with the old enemy to avoid the anger of a king who was not a Pharaoh but the one reigning in Jerusalem.

Then we see what the powerful can get up to for we now see Herod seeking to destroy all the children of a certain age, and Matthew intends us to remember the Pharaoh of the beginning of the Book of Exodus. Now we are stunned witnesses of the "anger of the mighty", as the state authorities, with a kind of evil logic, set about destroying "all the children in Bethlehem and in all its district, of two years old and younger". There is something disgusting about this, and our disgust is enhanced by the calm way in which Matthew tells the story; but it is all dreadfully familiar to the ordinary people of many countries today.

Next comes the return: God is effortlessly in charge, and has Joseph on the move again; and Matthew completes the Exodus pattern with the powerfully evocative phrase "he entered the land of Israel".

This is an exodus accomplished in spite of the mighty of the world, as Matthew now reminds us; for he mentions Archelaos, who had succeeded his father but (remarkably enough) was even worse than him; but makes no mention of Philip (who was nicer). In other words, it is through the machinations of the powerful that Jesus comes at last to Nazareth, from which his mission is eventually to begin.

So it is a remarkable story that Matthew tells here, of God's action against the mighty and on behalf of the powerless. It is a story of great hope for precisely those who have no resources of their own, and in his own unique way, Matthew gives us glimpses of hope that are invisible to the powers of this world: in particular, there is the way he uses Scripture, presenting Jesus'coming-to-be as a new Exodus, and quoting Hosea 11:1: "Out of Egypt I have called my son", which in its original context referred to God's fidelity; and even the quotation of Jeremiah 31:15 "Rachel mourning for her children, for they are not", strikes an unexpectedly cheerful note, for it comes from Jeremiah's so-called "Book of Consolation", and in that context carries a message of hope and optimism.

And Matthew ends his Christmas story, characteristically enough, with a quotation: *"he shall be called a Nazarene"*. Now Matthew's readers will not have needed telling that this is from Judges 13:5, where it refers to the birth of Samson; and they will have remembered that Samson too was to deliver Israel, and to die with outstretched hands, pulling down the pillars on which the house where the lords of the Philistines were. And they will have remembered the way that Jesus died, with arms outstretched, at the hands of the establishment. And there is further hope that Matthew gives, for he uses the "resurrection word" four times during his narrative, at verses 13,14,20, and 21, a foretaste of resurrection which neatly frames the account of Herod's homicidal anger, and offers the comforting reflection that the oppressive powers will not win in the end. In many countries today it is not difficult to pick up Matthew's clues, and to find in the text the grim situation of those who are at the bottom of the heap.

ii) *The Lucan Infancy Narratives*

Luke's stories of Jesus' infancy are the ones that we tend to think of first at Christmastime; and they too, although in a quite different way from Matthew's, demand to be read "from below", as we shall see.

a) A nod in the direction of the powerful

First, though, it is worth noting a trick that Luke plays on us; for he starts each of his first three chapters with what might be called "a nod in the direction of the powerful". The gospel, like its sequel, Acts, starts with a prologue addressed to *kratiste Theophile*. Now it is not exactly clear who this is meant to be, but the form of address is that reserved for the *equites*, the second rank of Roman society (where the wealthiest people tended to be found); and then Luke continues with a reference to another decidedly powerful person: "in the days of Herod the King", and immediately takes us, not to the palaces of the powerful, but to a charming couple who have stepped straight out of the pages of the Old Testament, Zachariah and Elisabeth.

The evangelist performs a similar sleight-of-hand at the beginning of chapter 2, when we read:

> *It happened in those days*
> *a decree went out from Caesar Augustus for the whole world*
> *to be enrolled*
> *This took place as the first census*
> *when Quirinius was legate of Syria,*

which might leave us thinking that Luke wants us to concentrate on the Roman Emperor and his most powerful local representative. And the evangelist does the same at the beginning of chapter 3:

> *In the 15th year of the reign of Tiberius Caesar*
> *when Pontius Pilatus was procurator of Judaea*
> *and Herod was tetrarch of Galilee,*
> *and Philip his brother was tetrarch of Iturea*
> *and the region of Trachonitis,*
> *and Lysanius was tetrarch of Abilene,*
> *in the High Priesthood of Annas and Caiaphas.*

This list sounds very solemn and historical; but Luke often fools us by starting with people he is not really interested in. All these important people are mentioned only to be dismissed. As we dismiss them, we note in passing that, powerful as they might be, they represent as unholy a collection of rogues as you might want to meet on a dark night. And what Luke is really interested in emerges only at the end of this list, when he writes "the word of God came to John son of Zechariah in the desert". So we must learn to look out for the people who *really* matter.

b) The people who *really* matter

After the historical preface, Chapter 1 of the gospel gives us two Annunciation stories, and a tale that links them (the visitation), followed by the birth of John the Baptist. The whole chapter is alive with people with whom we feel instantly at home. The very names of Zachariah ("the Lord has remembered") and Elisabeth ("my God has sworn") are posted as flags to indicate that we have left the empire of the powerful and entered the world of the 'anawim of the Old Testament. The fact that Elisabeth is descended from Aaron merely confirms this impression. More than that, they are among the marginalised, for, like Abraham and Sarah, or Elkanah and Hannah, they are barren. So we know that there will be a happy ending, for these are just the sort of people that God cannot let down. It is not surprising that the offspring of their union is to be called John ("God has acted graciously"). All this has a decidedly warming effect, after the chill induced by the mention of Herod at the beginning of the story.

Mary, on the other hand, is not an Old Testament figure, as Luke presents her; although we note the allusions to Is 7:14 in verse 31. Her son is to be, not "great before the Lord", like John (verse 15), but "great . . . Son of the Most High . . . [sitting on] the throne of David his father, king over the House of Jacob for ever, and of his reign there shall be no end". Luke has made some very careful distinctions here: Jesus is different from John, though connected to him, and nothing at all to do with the powerful, such as Herod or a Roman emperor, although the titles bestowed on him would sit nicely on the more megalomaniac of that species. Luke is deliberately asserting that the powerful of this world are simply irrelevant to the plan of God.

The visitation, the tale that links the two annunciations, has as its climax the Magnificat, a thoroughly revolutionary song of the 'anawim. There are those who find themselves asking why this song was not banned in South Africa during the state of emergency. It is a song that the establishment should tremble when they hear.

The first chapter of Luke's gospel is therefore a story of ordinary Old Testament folk, who have nothing to do with the whims of the mighty, but show fidelity to prayer, and experience fear and wonder at the presence of God. The whole story is told in a Semitised Greek, quite different from what Luke normally uses, which creates a wonderful atmosphere, and tells us that all will work out for these poor people. It is also thoroughly subversive of those who hold power.

c) Luke chapter 2: The Creation of Atmosphere

Thanks to Luke's skill in depicting a mood, we already approach this chapter in a certain frame of mind. He has painted a picture into which we can stroll, and of which we can become a part.

Luke 2:1-7 The Effects of Caesar's Decree

After the three-card trick of the opening verses, Luke brings our attention away from the irrelevant people who rule the world to the people who really matter to him. In verses 4-5, the focus is first on Joseph, then on Mary, concluding with the information that she is engaged to Joseph *and* pregnant. This is as jarring a piece of information in Greek as it is in English.

Verses 6-7 stress the helplessness of this odd couple, in profound contrast to, and in the face of, the control exercised by Augustus and Quirinius. It is hard to say what is really going on, because Luke does not give us sufficient details, but we learn that Mary and Joseph were unable to plan where the child might be born : "it happened when they were there the days were fulfilled for her to give birth and she brought forth her son, the first-born, and she wrapped him in linen cloths, and laid him in a manger". And when we hear that familiar word "manger", we nod wisely and say "Ah yes - a manger", for we have heard and sung the words since we were children; but if we were reading the text attentively, we should be leaping from our seats and shouting: "a *what?*" for a manger is a trough that animals eat from, and Luke means us to meditate on the plight of a mother who has to put her new-born child in a dog-bowl, "because there was no room in the dwelling-place". And with that line, Luke places the couple and their baby in solidarity with all refugees, all over the world. In South Africa today there are many people who can identify with this story.

Luke 2:8-14: God's presence to the marginalised

And, as we read the text "from below", we start to notice the cast of characters for the event that really matters: here where Jesus is born, there are no rulers or legates. Instead, we have shepherds, who in the ancient world were shady characters, decidedly on the margins of society; and we find that they are being addressed, remarkably enough, by angels, or, more precisely, "the angel of the Lord and the glory of the Lord", which, of course, is Old Testament code for God in person. And what is being offered by God to these offscourings of society is joy, glory, fear, and good news for all the people, all of which are authentic signs of the presence of God to God's people. Moreover, the shepherds are told of "a Saviour who is Christ the Lord in the City of David". You can hardly get grander than this, and, as has often been pointed out, the title represents a deliberate challenge to the notion that the Emperor Augustus is the Saviour of the world and the author of peace. In good scriptural manner, they are given a sign, which is simply a repetition of what we have already heard, that the child is "wrapped in swaddling-clothes" (this simply reflects the mother's care for the child), and lying in a manger (which probably carries an echo of the Greek version of Is 1:3). This is a remarkable inversion of the world's normal priorities, and, if read properly, should elicit a wild cheer from those who hear the story in a South African township, or in any place where people are pushed to the edges of society.

Luke 2:15-21: focus on the baby

In the first chapter of the gospel, Luke brought together two stories, those of John and Jesus, by means of the story of the visitation; now in the second chapter, he brings together the story of Mary, Joseph, and the child, with that of the scruffy layabouts who are chosen to be the recipients of the good news. We note the astonishment of the people, which is code, telling us that God is at work in this unlikely setting. We should take aboard also the fact that Mary is said to "contemplate". This is a sign to the reader, who is clearly meant to "do a Mary" at this point, and meditate on the significance of these things; or there would be no point in saying it: Luke is inviting us to think about how *we* should read the story and make it our story.

Now the shepherds are deftly removed from our sight, rather improbably praising God. Then the story that began with the Annunciation to Mary (1:31) is ended with the circumcision and the naming of the child as Jesus, or "Saviour". And all the time, the attentive reader is aware of the startling absence of those powerful figures who were named at the beginning of the chapter. We are bathed in the warmth or "rightness" of the story that Luke tells; and it would be a good deal less warm and less right if the powerful had got their grubby paws on the script. For God, the evangelist is telling us, does not operate in the way the world operates. The good news is good news for everyone; for the poor it implies liberation, and for the wealthy it also implies liberation. But the liberation of the wealthy is a more challenging one, less earnestly sought for.

Luke now brings his Christmas stories artistically to their ending, balancing the opening tales of the gospel with the tale of another charming old couple. Like Zachariah and Elisabeth, Simeon and Hanna have walked straight out of the pages of the Old Testament. On the scale of emperors and procurators they are wholly unimportant, but to Luke far more interesting: it is to such as these that the message of God is addressed.

Lastly, Luke leaves Jesus' infancy with yet another very attractive tale, which has Jesus "in the midst of the teachers", and "in his Father's house" or "on his Father's business". Significantly, Luke does not place Jesus among the "Scribes and Pharisees", for in the story of Jesus' life they will represent the opposition. So the second chapter of Luke ends as the first chapter began (and as the last chapter will end), in the Temple, among those who are prepared to listen to God, even when God speaks in unexpected ways. There are many people all over the world today, for whom this is extraordinarily good news.

We very properly wish each other a "happy Christmas". If, though, we can learn to read the Christmas stories as those stories demand to be read, through the eyes of the poor, then, wherever we are in the world today, we shall stand a far better chance of having that wish come true.

Chapter 4

The Beatitudes

We have just been looking at the way in which Matthew and Luke use the stories of Jesus' birth and childhood to image the values by which the adult Jesus was to live. The Beatitudes, which we consider next, are an expression of God's values, as Jesus lived them out and spoke them in the world of his time. They have to do with the business of building God's Reign, that oasis of justice and peace that might be termed the "contrast society", because it is so different from the society that we seem to live in. As in South Africa we try to build a new country, or as you work for the Kingdom of God in whatever country you live, we ask: what kind of a society does God want? In any country, the Beatitudes offer a kind of blue-print for what God's society should look like.

i) The world of the Beatitudes

Before looking at the society that Jesus wanted, it may be as well to try and give a brief account of the society in which he lived. Without bothering too much about details, I shall offer a broad picture, and as you read it, you should be able to ask: is my country like this? To that question the answer is almost certainly that it is if you look "from below", from the point of view of those at the bottom of the heap, or on the margins of society, precisely those people for whom the Beatitudes offer hope.

The Near East has always been a place where cultures clashed: Egyptians and Hapiru, Israel and Canaan, Assyria, Babylon, Jews and Greeks, Jews and Romans, Judaeans and Galileans, Judaeans and Samaritans; and, of course, it is still the same today. Jesus lived in that world of clashing cultures. In particular, Jesus' world was marked by what Alexander the Great had done, three hundred years earlier. His policy of tolerance for native cultures, which he had perhaps learnt from his tutor Aristotle, was a master-stroke, and had the effect of making his cherished Hellenistic (or Greek) civilisation acceptable, because it was not seen as a threat to nationalist sentiments. In Jesus' day Hellenism, which expressed itself in the user-friendly Greek language that had spread round the Mediterranean, was supreme. This was partly because it carried social and economic benefits, so that you could do business, both commercial and political, all round the Roman Empire if you knew Greek. Partly, too, it was attractive because of its attractive accomplishments: the Greek civilisation had given the world great art, literature, philosophy, science, including engineering science. It was also attractive because it was universal, so that if you were at home in that culture you could be at ease almost anywhere in the world. Most of all, perhaps, it was attractive because it was dominant, and people like backing winners. On the other hand, the Jewish culture and religion had never died; and as a matter of fact in a Greek setting it had taken on new and vigorous forms, which enabled it to face the challenges that lay ahead. So Jesus lived in a world of cultures that might either clash disastrously, or cohabit in a state of "creative tension".

Herod the Great, who probably died not long after Jesus was born, realised the strength of both the Jewish culture and the Greek. So he tried to keep the best of both worlds, building cities after the Greek style, and giving them names like Tiberias or Caesarea to please those in power in Rome. At the same time he tried hard to court the Jewish vote, by marrying into the Hasmonean dynasty (the descendants of the great liberation movement of the Maccabees), and by rebuilding the Temple in the grand manner; the Temple as he rebuilt it was utterly beautiful (they remembered centuries later how you could see the reflection of its marble from the coast). He was, however, never really accepted by the Jews; they did not care for his murderous tactics, and in any case his mother was not Jewish and therefore neither was he. His sons, except for Philip, were equally unsuccessful, and the situation was complicated by Roman imperial insensitivity. The lid was kept on the pressure-cooker only by strong military pressure, and by keeping an eye on likely subversives. This was a world that many people today would find familiar.

Communication in Palestine was excellent if you travelled on the main roads, which were skilfully engineered and had guaranteed security. Travelling on minor roads, however, was more dangerous: the roads were worse, and there was liable to be trouble from criminal elements. The authorities did not really bother with protecting the poorer classes or wasting good roads on them. So when Jesus told a story about a man who was mugged on the Jericho road, he was talking of a world that his hearers knew well. Sea travel was faster, but uncertain, and you were trusting yourself to the gods, as navigation was a bit haphazard, and weather-prediction even more of a matter for guess-work than it is today. The postal service was good for Roman citizens, non-existent for ordinary people.

In Rome itself, wandering about at night was unsafe: you might either be mugged or beaten up by the police. The wealthy of the land were very wealthy, normally because of their immense land-holdings, while the poor could be very poor; absentee landlords were common in Palestine, and this added to the social tensions. We find these absentee landlords surfacing in some of Jesus' parables.

There was also racial tension: difficulties between Jews and Greeks constantly exploded into violence; and since the Romans were the dominant power, tension between them and just about everyone else was exceedingly common. Considerable social divisions existed within Palestine itself: there is the gap between urban and rural, between slave and free, between the priestly aristocracy of the Sadducees, and the lay scholars called Pharisees. The picture one forms is of a very fragmented society. In response to this fragmentation, the Essenes, if they were really the people who set up house at Qumran, at the top end of the Dead Sea, determined on separation from impure outsiders. The revolutionary prophets, on the other hand, and those violent terrorists who come under the umbrella title of "Zealots", commanded hatred of outsiders on their adherents. So Jesus' policy, of talking to absolutely everybody, must have come as quite a shock; he actually forbade the hatred of outsiders.

Jesus' world was therefore a world like ours, one that was not as it should be, gripped by a system that begot both oppressors and oppressed. This means, of course, that the world to which the beatitudes were delivered is our world. So we can't evade the issue and say "that was then, and we are now". We need to ask: how do you read them, how do you teach them, and how do you live them in this country today? And, of course, they are thoroughly uncomfortable documents for most of us; but when the poor hear them proclaimed, they throw their hats into the air and cheer, for they are good news for the poor.

ii) Luke's beatitudes

We start with the Lucan version of the beatitudes, which you will find in Luke at 6:17-26. The reason for starting with them is that they have suffered a kind of "benign neglect" at the hands of Christian readers, and as you read them and reflect on them you can usefully ask why they are so little read in comparison with Matthew's version. I have done a translation of the passage, but it would be good for you to have a Bible open at the same time. It goes like this :

> And going down with them, he stood on a flat place
> and a great crowd of his disciples with him,
> and a great multitude of the people from all Judaea
> and Jerusalem and the Tyre and Sidon seashore

who came to hear him and be healed of their diseases
and those who were annoyed by impure spirits were healed

And the whole crowd sought to touch him,
because power came forth from him
and he healed all.

And he lifting up his eyes to his disciples said:

Congratulations to the destitute,
for yours is the Reign of God.

Congratulations to those who are hungry now,
for you shall be sated.

Congratulations to those who weep now,
for you shall laugh.

Congratulations when people hate you
and when they excommunicate you
and revile you
and cast out your name as evil because of the Son of Man.

Rejoice in that day and leap about,
for, see, your reward is great in heaven.
For in just the same way did those ancestors of theirs
to the prophets.

BUT

Woe to you who are rich, for you receive your comfort.
Woe to you who are filled now, for you will be hungry.
Woe to you who laugh now, for you will mourn and weep.
Woe to you when all speak well of you.
For in just the same way did those ancestors of theirs to the false prophets.

So it starts charmingly enough: we see the picture of Jesus "going down with them", expressing a solidarity with people. And we see who is with him: he is surrounded by absolutely everyone, disciples, crowds from Judaea and Jerusalem, and even, for Luke is the evangelist of the Church's great push outwards to the nations, "the Tyre and Sidon seashore" (foreigners, that is to say)! We notice, too, that Luke mentions especially those in greatest need, "who came to hear him and be healed of their diseases, and those who were annoyed by impure spirits were healed"; and Luke stresses their enthusiasm: "And the whole crowd sought to touch him, because power came forth from him and he healed all". It is a good picture, this, and we bask in Jesus' success, and in his openness to the marginalised and to the Gentiles.

Then however, like a cold shower, comes his teaching. He is evidently seated, the correct position for a rabbi, for he "lifts up his eyes to his disciples". And this is what they must have been astonished to hear:

> *Congratulations to the destitute,*
> *for yours is the Reign of God.*

These are quite startling words, which turn upside down the values of our world, and even the values of those bits of the Old Testament that equated godliness and prosperity. The syntax, too, contributes to the sense of shock, for it starts with a kind of political slogan, in the third person: "happy are the poor", and then switches to addressing them in the second person: "for yours is God's kingdom". And so it goes on, for verse after astonishing verse, Jesus congratulating the starving, the ones who weep, and those who are hated, excommunicated, reviled, and slandered for Jesus' sake. Most remarkable of all is Jesus' advice to those who suffer in this way. You and I would call on our lawyers if unpleasant things got said about us, but Jesus tells them instead to "Rejoice in that day and leap about, for, see, your reward is great in heaven. For in just the same way did those ancestors of theirs to the prophets". And when, as we come to the end of this list, we find ourselves asking "can he possibly be serious?" it is with an awful feeling that this is just what he is being.

Then, as though we have not been sufficiently battered, there comes another list, but not of congratulations this time. It starts with the word "but", which just occasionally for Luke is a word of such importance that you really ought to print it "BUT". And this jumbo-sized "but" introduces the second half of Luke's beatitudes, which are not beatitudes at all, but go like this:

> *Woe to you who are rich, for you receive your comfort.*
> *Woe to you who are filled now, for you will be hungry.*
> *Woe to you who laugh now, for you will mourn and weep.*
> *Woe to you when all speak well of you.*
> *For in just the same way did those ancestors of theirs.*
> *to the false prophets.*

As is the case quite often in Luke, this is thoroughly subversive of the established order, and suggests a completely different way of seeing reality from that which is presented to us by the television set. We are being invited to see everything, not through the eyes of those who are important, "from above", but through the eyes of the marginalised, "from below".

iii) Matthew's beatitudes

You will find Matthew's slightly different version at 5:1-12, and you might like to check what your Bibles say against the following version:

*And seeing the crowds he went up into the mountain
And when he sat down his disciples came to him.*

And opening his mouth he taught them, saying

*Congratulations to the poor in spirit,
for theirs is the reign of heaven.*

*Congratulations to those who mourn,
for they shall be comforted.*

*Congratulations to the gentle,
for they shall inherit the earth.*

*Congratulations to those who hunger and thirst for justice,
for they shall be sated.*

*Congratulations to the merciful,
for they shall be mercied.*

*Congratulations to the pure in heart,
for they shall see God.*

*Congratulations to the peace-makers,
for they shall be called children of God.*

*Congratulations to those who are persecuted
for the sake of justice,
for theirs is the reign of heaven.*

*Congratulations to you when they revile you
and persecute
and say every evil thing against you
falsely on my account.*

*Rejoice and be glad,
for your reward is great in heaven.*

For so they persecuted your predecessors as prophets.

This version is of course much better known, and if I asked you to recite the beatitudes, it is Matthew's that you would attempt to stumble through. You might, by the way, just ask yourself why this should be so. It is partly, I suspect, because they seem at first blush less harsh than Luke's version; but it is also because Matthew is a gifted teacher, and writes memorable phrases. All of us, for example, have by heart Matthew's version of the Lord's Prayer, but if I asked you to recite Luke's version, the chances are that you would pretend not to hear. Matthew's Beatitudes have a kind of magical quality, which survives even in translation, and we are seduced by the magic, but interestingly there is strikingly little agreement among scholars on how they should be taken. It is sometimes said that the first beatitude sets the tone, and once you have grasped what that is about there is not much to say about the rest of them. You can make up your mind as to whether you agree with this verdict.

It is worth noting where Matthew sets the beatitudes. As in Luke, there are crowds, but we get the strong impression that the crowds drive Jesus up the mountain, and that this teaching is reserved for the disciples. Secondly, the Mountain reminds us inevitably of Sinai, where Moses received the Law; Matthew at several point in his gospel presents Jesus as the new Moses; but the difference here, of course, is that Moses *received* the Law on the Mountain, whereas Jesus is *giving* the Law. Also, of course, in ancient traditions, mountains are places where the gods live, holy places where humans encounter the divine. Then, in an authoritative gesture, he tells them to sit down. Now Matthew gives a very formal beginning to the discourse, which is much longer, of course, than just the Beatitudes, for we are starting here the whole of the Sermon on the Mount, which takes up chapters 5 to 7 of Matthew's gospel. Matthew marks the start of the address in three separate ways: "opening his mouth", "taught", and "saying", thereby ensuring that we are listening very carefully indeed before Jesus starts.

Some scholars argue that what Matthew is doing here is to tell Israel how to be Israel, drawing on its rich resources, to live the life of God's *'anawim*. Because God is who God is, the real Israel must behave in certain ways, which they already know about from the Old Testament. If they do this, then they have grounds for confidence. So the basic slogan is: be Israel, be faithful to the Jewish revelation, and all will be well. And as we read the beatitudes in this country today, the answer to our problems are not far to seek: all we have to do is to live out what they command, and God will not let us down. A way of checking how well each of us reads the beatitudes is to ask ourselves: who do I really think is blessed, or happy, or worthy of congratulation?

In many ways, the beatitudes are a kind of commentary on that text in Isaiah 61, which Luke put at the beginning of Jesus' mission, in his account of the episode in the synagogue in Nazareth, about bringing "good news to the poor". And it might be useful just to read through the first four verses of Isaiah 61, with Matthew's version of the Beatitudes open in front of you, just to see how many echoes you can detect. But there are other Old Testament echoes as well of this notion that God is particularly on the side of the poor. Look at Proverbs 16:19, for example: "better to be of a lowly spirit among the poor, than to divide the spoil with the proud", or Proverbs 29:23: "A person's pride will bring humiliation, but one who is lowly in spirit will obtain honour". And you get the same sort of idea in the Psalms, for example, at 34:18: "The Lord is near to the broken-hearted, and saves the crushed in spirit". And in the literature that Jews composed after the books that made up their Bible we find other echoes, in the Psalms of Solomon, for example, or in this passage from the War Scroll at Qumran :

> *"after the battle is over:*
> *He has taught war [to the hand of] the feeble*
> *and steadied the trembling knee;*
> *he has braced the back of the smitten*
> *Among the poor in spirit [there is power].*

> *And by the perfect of way all the gentiles of wickedness*
> *shall be destroyed (1QM 14:6-7).*

So when Matthew has Jesus insist on the happiness of the poor in spirit, he is simply going back to a notion that is already in the Old Testament, and to ideas that were part of the air a contemporary Jew would breathe. The concept of the "poor in spirit" refers to those who look to God for everything. It does not allow any of the common evasions, that poverty is somehow the fault of the poor, or that poverty is good, or that we're all really poor, or that it is alright to be rich. All these are ways of ducking the challenge of the Beatitudes. The essential element is that of total dependence on God. Notice how carefully Matthew balances the first and the eighth beatitude:

> *Congratulations to the poor in spirit,*
> *for theirs is the reign of heaven,*

and

> *Congratulations to those who are persecuted*
> *for the sake of justice,*
> *for theirs is the reign of heaven.*

What Matthew is saying, in other words, is that the reign of God belongs equally to the poor in spirit and to those who are persecuted for justice's sake. They are therefore presumably the same group. Note Matthew's characteristic emphasis on the demands of justice in this last beatitude: there is no room for complacency here, any more than there is in the first beatitude.

The second beatitude is a beautiful one:

> *Congratulations to those who mourn,*
> *for they shall be comforted.*

Once again there is an echo of our passage from Isaiah (61:2). The point here is that all misery can be coped with because God is present where God is needed. Notice how, as with all the beatitudes, the message is for those who most need it.

The next beatitude is simply astonishing. It reads:

> *Congratulations to the gentle,*
> *for they shall inherit the earth.*

The people who are congratulated here are those at the bottom of the heap. The word for those who are to be congratulated is often translated "meek", thereby eliciting the cynical tailpiece "if that's alright with the rest of you". But it is nothing to do with being a doormat to everyone else; nor is it a matter of assumed meekness, like those Ancient Greeks who tried by appropriately meek behaviour to avoid the charge of *hybris*, that kind of arrogance of the mighty which according to Greek philosophy could rouse the anger of the gods, or of secular rulers. A more likely way of understanding this beatitude is Ps 37:11, where the point is simply not to worry about the apparent prosperity of the wicked. The Hebrew word here is *'anawim*, that group specially favoured by God, whom we have already mentioned.

Next comes a beatitude that shows Matthew's characteristic concern for justice, that OldTestament virtue which implied getting everything into its right relation, without which no peace was possible:

> *Congratulations to those who hunger and thirst for justice,*
> *for they shall be sated.*

A powerful promise, this, that those who hunger and thirst for God's good order will be, not just fed, as you might have expected, but *sated*. Justice, for which Matthew's word is *dikaiosune*, is God's final act. Have a look at Psalm 107:5, 8-9, which is all about God's faithfulness in bringing the people back from exile. And it is worth making the point that the beatitudes are really not so much about what we are to do or how we are to live, as about the action of God (which of course has consequences for how we must live). Justice will come, is the promise, and our part is to "hang on in there". Always provided, of course, that we are really hungering and thirsting for it.

Next comes a beatitude that Matthew put into dramatic form in the parable of the Unforgiving Servant (see 18:23-25 if you can't remember what that is):

> *Congratulations to the merciful,*
> *for they shall be mercied.*

Once again, this is a profoundly Old Testament notion: the Greek version of Proverbs 17:5, for example, reads:

> *the one who laughs at the poor will provoke his Maker,*
> *the one who rejoices over the one being destroyed will not be unpunished;*
> *the one who has bowels of compassion will be mercied.*

Both here and in translating Matthew, I have used a rather odd English word "mercied", to indicate that the same word is used in both parts of this beatitude. It is the same verb that we used to sing when asking for mercy on our sinfulness at mass: the Greek for "Lord Have Mercy" is *Kyrie Eleison*, and that is the word, connected with the oil poured on wounds, and with our word "alms", that Matthew uses here.

The sixth beatitude is different again: it offers the possibility of people actually seeing God, which the Old Testament knew was not really an option for human beings, or at best thoroughly dangerous: see, for example, the striking story of Moses at Exodus 33:18-23, or for the terror induced by the sight of God, Manoah's reaction at Judges 13:22. But our beatitude leaps past all that, for it reads:

> *Congratulations to the pure in heart,*
> *for they shall see God.*

Those who are going to do this impossible thing are those described in Psalm 24 as permitted to go into the Temple: "those who have clean hands and pure hearts". This refers, that is to say, to the inner person, as against outward acts, and is a matter of our basic attitude.

Next, we read of the peace-makers:

> *Congratulations to the peace-makers,*
> *for they shall be called children of God.*

I have tried to use the inclusive term "children", instead of "sons", as Matthew wrote. There are good reasons for doing this; but it could lead us to overlook the point that Matthew's term carries the notion of "angels", those who were "sons of God" in Genesis 6:2. For Jesus' group, these would be the people who address God as "Abba", in that extraordinary term which the early Christians never forgot, even when they started to talk Greek. The peace-makers are those who are engaged in building "Shalom", the lovely Hebrew word, which means not so much an absence of war as peace with God, which depends on just relationships. It is that quality that we are short of in this country today. It is also a quality that is quite unmistakable when you find it; without it you simply cannot build a society that will last.

The next beatitude we have already looked at when we considered the first one:

> *Congratulations to those who are persecuted*
> *for the sake of justice,*
> *for theirs is the reign of heaven.*

It is not too fanciful to detect here the situation of Matthew's church, in those who are persecuted. Matthew is explaining to them that they have not made some kind of terrible mistake, but that this is always what you must expect if you live out gospel values.

The next beatitude is thought by many to be a late addition to the list:

> *Congratulations to you when they revile you*
> *and persecute*
> *and say every evil thing against you*
> *falsely on my account.*

Luke has more or less the same of course, and the addition of

> *Rejoice and be glad,*
> *for your reward is great in heaven.*
> *For so they persecuted your predecessors as prophets.*

is in both lists.

iv) Conclusions

a)   The first conclusion, obviously, is that here we have two lists of beatitudes, different in some respects from each other, but clearly with the same tone; and, as far as we can see, they come ultimately from the same source. The lists present the values of the kingdom that Jesus came to proclaim. One useful exercise might be to see what kind of list you could produce if you were asked to draw up a list of the world's values. It might, I suppose, go something like this (but you could no doubt do much better):

> *Congratulations to the powerful*
> *the rich*
> *the well-connected*
> *the educated*
> *those with two cars*
> *and two houses*
> *those who get their retaliation in first*
> *those who have never known suffering*
> *those who buy everything they see in the TV advertisements*
> *those who do not mind whom they trample in their rush to get on*
> *those whom everyone speaks well of.*

b) What are we to make of the differences between Luke and Matthew? Quite simply, I think, that they are writing for two different situations. Luke is asking the question: "who is the good news for?" and is concerned above all, perhaps because he is writing for a wealthy and settled church, with expressing the economic implications of conversion. Matthew, on the other hand, is writing in a situation of persecution, where there is not nearly so much money around, and is much more interested in the question: "how should disciples behave?" So in Matthew's beatitudes what we are given, in effect, is a "portrait of Jesus", on which disciples are to model their behaviour, whereas Luke is much more interested in the "portrait of the true disciple".

My esteemed colleague Fr Emmanuel Lafont suggests, in a characteristically telling couple of phrases, that where Luke has a "problem with money", Matthew and his church have "an attitude problem". So, if you look at Luke, you find those characters in chapters 1 and 2 who are held up for our admiration; and, as we have seen, they are very decidedly not the rich and powerful. It is Luke alone who gives us the parable of the Rich Fool (12:13-21), or the "dishonest steward" (16:1-13), or describes the Pharisees as "lovers of money" (16:14), or tells us of Lazarus and the Rich Man (16:19-31, which is really the beatitudes and woes presented by Luke in the dramatic form of a parable). It is Luke who gives us Zacchaeus' extravagant generosity as the sign of his conversion, the apostles insisting on giving something more precious than "silver and gold" at Acts 3:6; or the "communism" of the early church at 4:32-37, or the solemn little tale of Ananias and Sapphira at 5:1-11. And so on: read through the whole of Luke and Acts, and make your own list of places where Luke shows his reservations about money.

Matthew, on the other hand, is much more concerned about the disciples not losing their correct attitude. That comes out clearly in the parable of salt and light, at 5:13-14, or the teaching on anger against a brother (5:22-24), or the "antitheses" in the Sermon on the Mount ("you have heard it said . . . but I say to you . . ."), where the words of the Law are contrasted with the correct inner attitude of one who would follow Jesus; or the teaching in the same Sermon about justice, almsgiving and fasting. Or see how the following parables are all to do with getting a right attitude: the buried treasure (13:44); the pearl of great price (13:45-46); the dragnet (13:47-50); the workers in the vineyard (20:1-16); the wedding feast (22:1-14); the two sons (21:28-32); the ten virgins (25:1-13); the sheep and the goats (25:31-46); or, finally, the evidence of tension in Matthew's church that you find scattered throughout chapter 18.

So the differences between the two lists of those who are to be congratulated are not really enormous, and almost certainly reflect the different situations of the two churches for whom the two gospels were written. The question that *we* have to face, if the gospel is to come into our lives, is this: who in this country today are those who are in fact congratulated? And the next question is: who in this country today are those to whom the Lord would cry "woe"? If we propose to live out our gospel discipleship, it is essential not to run away from the challenge.

Chapter 5

Reading the

Passion Narratives

There are really just three points that I should like to make in this chapter, and they can serve as the three "pegs" on which to hang the texts I want to read in the course of it. The three points are the following:

i) Killing is a deceptively easy way out. In any country, and certainly in South Africa, there is a tendency to see killing as a solution, to cope with tension by disposing of those uncomfortable human beings who apparently cause the tension. However, killing never achieves what its perpetrators think it will, because human nature and human society are not constructed that way, and, in one way or another, you pay for killing others.

ii) It is important for victims to remember the pain. Our tendency is to forget it, and pretend it never happened. This is true both for those who cause the pain and for the victims.

iii) There is no point in telling the story in which we remember the pain, unless there is hope. And there is a corollary to this: even telling the story is, for victims and perpetrators alike, an act of hope.

We can take these points one by one.

i) Killing is a deceptively easy way out

In South Africa today, we are living in a country where people have been taught that the way to deal with opponents is to kill them. It is idle to seek to establish who is to blame for this literally diabolical situation, sufficient merely to note that it is so, and that those who kill are doing the work of the devil, and dealing with counter-human powers that are greater than they can possibly control, whatever it may feel like. So we have had the murder of Matthew Goniwe (and, as I write, we witness an undignified scramble to deny responsibility for that event - another characteristic of evil), and of Steve Biko, and of Chris Hani, and countless others who have been killed and maimed for reasons that must have seemed sufficient to those who ordered the violence and perhaps to those who actually did the deeds. It very often seems like a good idea, especially to those in "power" of one sort or another, to eliminate the inconvenient and discourage others.

However, it never works quite as such people might think, for there is a God, and that God is working in the darkest places of the human desert to nurture life and counter evil. So the name of Steve Biko speaks louder in his death than it ever did in his lifetime; the murder of Chris Hani deprived the ANC of an important strategist, but, if anything, advanced the negotiations that it was surely intended to halt. Archbishop Romero's assassination while he said mass focused the indignation of the world, and brought nearer the end of the Salvadorean oligarchy who had caused him to be killed. And the same is true of the demented killings at Slagtersnek in 1816, or Soweto in 1976, or wherever else people opt for the counter-human solution of the demonic powers.

Naturally, for us who read the gospels with the eyes of faith, those same forces were at work in bringing about the death of Jesus. It must have seemed to them an obvious move to make, but they fell into the trap. Paul diagnoses their failure in 1 Corinthians (as part of his attempt to persuade the Corinthian church to come back to unity), when he writes:

> *none of the rulers of this world recognised*
> *[the glory that God had planned for us];*
> *for if they had recognised it,*
> *they would not have crucified the Lord of glory (1 Corinthians 2:8).*

And when you look at the gospels, this is precisely what you find, the powers half-understanding what they do, plotting to remove an inconvenience, but not really having full insight into the game that was afoot. So Mark starts his passion-narrative in this arresting way:

> *And it was the Passover and the Unleavened Bread after two days,*
> *and the Chief Priests and the Scribes*
> *were seeking how they might take him by a trick*
> *and kill him.*
>
> *For they were saying: not at the festival,*
> *lest there should be a tumult of the people.*

Mark tells us that the Chief Priests and Scribes are on the point of starting the greatest festival of the year, and we might piously suppose them to be preparing to celebrate it worthily. A Catholic priest, for example, would be wondering about the choir and the altar servers and whether he can remember where he put everything from last year, and how things will go in the services, and, no doubt, whether he is spiritually prepared for the feast. Not so these characters, however; they are contemplating skulduggery (*"by a trick"*) and murder. Above all, like so many of those in "power", they are anxious to avoid unnecessary fuss: *"lest there should be a tumult of the people"*. So the plan is to avoid killing Jesus at the festival; this is not, however, out of reverence for this very great feast, but to avoid civil disorder at a traditionally volatile moment. Now seeing what they are about does not entitle us to mock at them, for gospel is always our story and not a story of long ago; and we are quite as capable as they of behaving in this way. For the moment, simply notice that they are opting for the easy way out, and, in so doing, betraying their integrity as the religious establishment of the nation. Notice, too, that whatever they may suppose, they are not on the winning side. John's gospel makes this point in a slightly different way:

> *And one of them, Caiaphas, who was High Priest of that year, said to them:*
>
> *You know nothing,*
> *you do not think that it is of advantage to you*
> *that one man should die for the people,*
> *so that the whole nation should not be destroyed (John 11:49-50).*

Here, with a characteristic Johannine touch, the evangelist makes it clear that God's agenda and the agenda of the religious establishment were not the same. Caiaphas thought he was speaking in the interests of the establishment when he insisted on Jesus' death; but John comments, laconically but highly effectively, that

> *he said this, not of himself, but being high priest of that year he prophesied*
> *that Jesus was going to die on behalf of the people,*
> *and not on behalf of the people only,*
> *but also so that the scattered children of God*
> *might be gathered together into one (51-52).*

The establishment was right here, but for the wrong reasons.

ii) *The importance of remembering*

Let me introduce this section with an anecdote. Every year, at the seminary where I teach, we very properly celebrate Soweto Day, June 16th. In 1992 on that day I had been summoned to a teacher training college near Durban where I functioned as occasional chaplain. The college had recently gone multi-racial, and as Soweto Day approached tensions were rising: black students were threatening trouble if the day was not properly celebrated, while some white students, not seeing why they should be prevented from attending lectures (rather unusual students, you may reflect!) were making plans to patrol the campus; and both sides were going to be armed and angry. So the college devised a form of religious service, and wheeled out some of us Christian ministers, who spoke of the significance of the day and why it was important for both sides to remember what had happened; and all went off peacefully enough.

The next year I discovered that I needed to be taught a lesson myself. Soweto Day came round, and we had a mass organised early in the morning; I found myself resenting slightly the time it would take up, and making excuses to myself that I had a thousand things to do. I would be there, of course, but arrived with hardly any time to spare, and found myself getting annoyed and bored (boredom is a frequent defence mechanism when we do not really want to get involved in something). The mass started outside, like Easter without the fire, as I muttered crossly to myself, and when we went inside I noticed that in front of the altar there were crossed sjamboks, which I immediately dismissed as "way over the top", and the paschal candle surrounded symbolically with barbed wire. But as I examined what was going on inside me, the realisation dawned that all these irritations of mine were really ways of keeping it all at a distance, probably because of the fear that I might be made to feel guilty for being white.

However then the mass proper started, and my mood started to alter (it generally does once mass starts!). Instead of the penitential rite with which the Catholic mass normally begins, four of our students gave testimony about the significance of the day. The first, in a deadpan voice which somehow heightened the emotion, simply reported the facts (chilling enough in themselves) of what happened in Soweto on June 16th 1976. The second was a white seminarian, who on that day was a businessman, and only discovered that something was amiss when he saw the faces of his black staff, as they asked him "have you heard?" He had not heard, and the discovery of what was going on where they lived was the start of the eye-opening process that led him to where he is today. The third and fourth witnesses were seminarians from Soweto who had been there on the day. The first of them had us chuckling at his memories of getting out of school as a 13-year-old, when the sisters forbade them to leave class, and the comrades insisted; then, just as we were seeing the funny side of their victory over the sisters, it was not funny any more, for he was relating how they got out of school and saw dead bodies everywhere, and other sights that 13-year-olds should not be asked to see. The final witness lost a cousin on that day, and had two brothers shot by the police, and was himself sjambokked. And he ended : "am I bitter? Of course I am, but bitterness is not enough - we must find our hope in Jesus". And it began to dawn on me as I listened that, of course, these were deeply painful memories that were being laid bare before us, painful for both blacks and whites; but that we served no purpose whatever by running away from the pain or trying to pretend that it had not happened.

Lastly there was an impassioned sermon, pleading for justice and democracy, from a white South African priest who recalled being in Auschwitz (a telling parallel, this) on Soweto Day a few years earlier, and how the tears coursed down his cheeks at the reminder of what human beings can do to one another. But we never learn unless we remember these things; and I came to realise, as I listened to all this, that it was painful for all who bore witness and painful for those who heard, but essential to remember, if there was to be any healing, what had happened on that day.

It is important, therefore, not to shirk the pain; and the early Christians were certainly unafraid to face the pain. Look, for example, at how Paul takes this particular bull by the horns:

> *For I decided to know nothing among you,*
> *except Jesus Christ and him crucified (1 Cor 2:2).*

Paul, that is to say, did not run away from the reality of the cross, even to so philosophically-minded a group as his Corinthians; he actually insisted on the cross as the centre of his message. And he even makes this very daring formulation:

> *I am crucified with Christ;*
> *I live, no longer I, but Christ in me (Galatians 2:19-20).*

This was daring, because Deuteronomy 21:23 explicitly pronounces accursed anyone who underwent the punishment of the cross, it seems:

> *Christ bought us back from the curse of the Law,*
> *having become a curse for our sakes,*
> *for it is written :*
> *"Cursed be everyone who hangs on a tree" (Gal 3:13).*

So Paul takes the worst that the enemies of the gospel could throw at him, and calmly acknowledges it, indeed makes it a proud boast. We must learn to do the same, and to read the message in our own lives.

Following Paul's example, the early Christians likewise steadfastly refused to shirk the pain. Mark's account of the Passion is perhaps the bleakest of all. It starts with the anointing at Bethany, when the unnamed woman is described as anointing Jesus "for my burial"(14:3-9); that story is framed by the account of the plot to put Jesus to death (1-2; 10-11). Then Mark proceeds with the account of that terrible supper, with its chilling sense of a meal that has gone terribly wrong. The Passover supper is for Jews the greatest possible celebration of community solidarity, and, incredibly, at this meal of all meals we hear predictions of betrayal (18,20, cf v.31). But in oriental society you do not under any circumstances betray those with whom you have eaten; so it is hard to imagine that things could get any worse.

Then Mark goes into the mysterious and troubling words : "take, this is my body . . . this is my blood of the covenant, which is poured out for many" (23-24).

After that, things get worse, and you can feel Mark "facing the pain", as he takes us into Gethsemane, and Jesus' terrible, but ultimately serene, prayer, uttered while the most favoured disciples snore. This is followed immediately by the arrest of Jesus, and the headlong flight of those who were with him: the last time we see the male disciples in the gospel, the view is obscured by the dust that their escape makes: "and abandoning him they fled, all of them" (14:50) is the grim comment Mark makes on their discipleship.

This is followed, of course, by the farce of a trial before the High Priest; but as we start that story, we are given a glimmer of hope in the shape of a glimpse of Peter: "and Peter followed [so he was, it seems a disciple after all!] from afar right inside into the hall of the High Priest,and he was sitting with the servants and warming himself in the direction of the fire" (54); but Mark only gives us that glimpse in order to tell us the dreadful and moving story that he places after the trial, which erupts in chaos and spitting and hitting in verse 65.

This is how the story goes:

And when Peter was below in the courtyard, there came one of the little slave-girls of the High Priest.

And seeing Peter warming himself,
looking at him she said:
You too were with the Nazarene, that Jesus.

And he denied it saying:
I neither know nor understand what you are saying.
And he went out outside into the forecourt.

And the little slave-girl seeing him began again to say to the bystanders:
This chap is one of them.

And he denied again.
And after a short time again the bystanders said to Peter:
In truth you are one of them,
for you are a Galilean.

But he began to curse and to swear:
I do not know the man you are talking about.

And immediately a second time cock crew.
And Peter remembered the word as Jesus had spoken to him:
Before the cock crows twice,
thrice you will deny me.
And he broke down and wept.

It is beautifully and unforgettably told, this story, and we shall linger on it a while. It starts with Peter, whom we have just seen trying to be a long-range disciple, still not quite there where the action is, but "below, in the courtyard". Then, with a deft gesture of contempt, Mark tells us who Peter's interlocutor is going to be: "one of the little slave-girls of the High Priest". Now the last thing that Peter said was that "even if all of them are made to trip up by you, I shan't be"; and here these brave words are put to the test by this not very frightening young lady.

She sees Peter "warming himself"; that is a neat touch by Mark, for you only warm yourself if you are cold, and Peter is cold with cowardice and treachery. Then she speaks the truth to him: she looks at him, to check that there is no case of mistaken identity here, and says, "You too were with the Nazarene, that Jesus". Brave Peter cannot face the truth; and as we listen to him blustering, we recall that just a few verses earlier Jesus remained silent (61) in the face of *false* witnesses, and here Peter is saying far too much, in the presence of someone who is telling the *truth*! Listen to the thoroughness of his denial : "I neither know nor understand what you are saying", and see how the denial is robbed of all conviction by what he does: "and he went outside into the forecourt", clearly running away from the truth.

The little girl, by contrast, is terrier-like in pursuit of the truth, and invokes the bystanders in support of her thesis. Peter denies again (as in Jesus' prayer in Gethsemane, so here, Mark is sparing in his account of the second out of the three parts of the episode), and then the bystanders give what they clearly regard as the climax of the case against Peter: "you are a Galilean". This has a really appalling effect on Peter, and we would much rather he had not spoken as he "began to curse and to swear: 'I do not know the man you are talking about'". It is impossible to feel anything but rather unwell as we read these words or hear them, but Mark resolves the crisis with economical skill: "and immediately a second time cock crew" [when was the first time? we ask, if we are feeling prosaic]; then Mark reports in full the significance of this: "and Peter remembered the word as Jesus had spoken to him: before the cock crows twice, thrice you will deny me". Finally, with the touch of a master composer, the story is brought to exactly the right conclusion: "and he broke down and wept". Nothing else needs to be said.

So Mark's story goes grimly on, facing the pain without flinching; next we come to Jesus' interrogation by Pilate, the story of how the crowd preferred Barabbas, the mockery of the soldiers, and the crucifixion, in a terrible parody of an enthronement ceremony, with the title "the King of the Jews", and his two co-regents on either side of his "throne". Then he dies, mocked by the passers-by, the high priests, and even his fellow-convicts, and even, apparently, by God, as he cries in his native Aramaic, "My God,

my God, why have you forsaken me?" Even that is not really understood, as
the bystanders think he was really calling on Elijah, and pause in their min-
istrations, to see if Elijah might come after all.

It is a bleak story that Mark tells, in which every detail is made to count;
but what we notice for our purpose is that at no stage does Mark, or the
church for which he was writing, seek to minimise the pain of this terrible
episode.

iii) There is no point in telling a story unless it gives you hope

However, we are not suppose to recall the pain for its own sake; that
would be masochism. Pain, though useful in our universe, is destructive
when unrelieved or not learnt from; and the reason for telling about the pain
is that it is important to remember where we have been, in order to know
where we are; but also in order to discern some light about where it is we
are going. And we see that dawning of hope also in the way the early Christians told the Passion story.

a) Signs of hope in Mark's Passion Narrative

So Paul, for example, hardly ever speaks of the cross of Jesus without
also mentioning Resurrection in the same breath. (I shan't give you references; you can chase through Paul, looking for the cross, and verifying - or
falsifying - this statement for yourself). Even in Mark's gospel, where none
of the pain is shirked, there are signs of hope. It is true that you have to look
for them, and it is true that for the most part they come only after the death
of Jesus; but they are there, nonetheless, if you look for them.

For example, we notice that Mark, who is not one for wasting words,
tells us at 15:21 that Simon the Cyrenian, who was "coming from the field"
and found himself conscripted to carry Jesus' cross, was "the father of Alexander and Rufus". Now there is no point in mentioning these names unless they are known to the church for whom Mark was writing; and why
should they be known to those early Christians unless something happened
to their father on that day when he became a convicted criminal's reluctant
assistant?

A further sign that Mark offers is the number of Old Testament quotations and allusions scattered throughout the narrative of Jesus' passion. There
is no need to point them out to you; if you get hold of a good modern translation of the Bible, they should be given in the marginal notes. The thing to
observe is what Mark is doing here by including them: it is code (such as his
readers would not have missed) for the affirmation that God is in control.
For if the Old Testament is being fulfilled, then this is not a random act of

utterly meaningless evil that we are witnessing. If you can find an Old Testament frame for it, then God is working, and the meaning will emerge.

After the death of Jesus, the signs of hope come thick and fast. At 15:33 we read of "darkness over the whole earth, from the sixth to the ninth hour", which we are presumably to interpret as God's comment on what is going on. Even more striking, however, is the centurion's comment at 15:39, which I regard as the climax of the whole gospel : "and the centurion who stood over against him, seeing that he expired in this way, said 'In truth, this man was son of God'". From the very beginning of the gospel (1:1) we have been told that Jesus was "son of God"; but we have spent the whole of the rest of the gospel learning what it means to have this lofty title. It means, in this specific instance, to die alone and apparently abandoned, and to be recognised, not by the religious establishment, nor by the disciples, but by the professional soldier who has seen a thousand criminals die in just this way. Mark is telling us that only when you stand at the foot of the cross can you understand what it means to call Jesus "son of God". It is, however, possible to make that affirmation, and to see it to be true. So this verdict by the centurion is a sign of the profoundest possible hope.

Once Jesus dies, too, we find that he has supporters after all. Not all that many, it is true, but at verses 40-41 we discover that the women are faithfully there "watching", and at the end of the chapter it is they who see where Jesus is laid. In addition there is a supporter of whom we have hitherto not heard, one Joseph of Arimathea, "a well-to-do counsellor", who "has the guts to go to Pilate and ask for the body of Jesus . . . and having purchased a shroud, taking him down wrapped him in the shroud, and placed him in a tomb which was carved out of the rock, and rolled a stone at the door of the tomb" (43-46).

b) The Passion Narrative in Matthew

Even in Mark, therefore there are signs of hope. Subsequent retellings, while never seeking to deny the pain, all show an increasing tendency to affirm the hope. In Matthew's gospel, for example you have one or two additions to show that Jesus was on the "right side", such as the (slightly vindictive) account of the suicide of Judas (27:3-9), Pilate's wife's dream, and Pilate's formal washing of the hands (27:19, 24), which sounds too much like Deuteronomy 21:6-9 to be entirely convincing for a Roman functionary. Matthew also has the legends about the earthquake and the opening of the tombs (27:51-52), and the posting of the guard (62-66). All of these reveal how much the early Christians have been meditating on the story of Jesus' death since Mark's account was written, and to what extent they are starting to see the bright side. The pain is still there, of course, but we are much more aware of the hope.

c) Luke's Passion Account

Luke's version is different again. For Luke, as you probably know, the passion comes at the mid-point of his two-volume story, which might be termed "the Acts of Jesus" and "the Acts of the early Church". Luke is writing for a church that finds itself at ease in the Graeco-Roman world, and has established itself all round the Mediterranean. Luke is temperamentally a far gentler evangelist, and all Mark's bleakness has vanished in consequence. Luke is also something of an artist with words, and presents us with unforgettable scenes like that deft touch of Jesus looking at Peter, after Peter's denial, which for Luke is what provokes Peter's tears (22:61). Luke also is the only one to have Jesus sent to Herod (23:6-12), and the only one to mention the consequent friendship between Herod and Pilate, which Luke manages to present as a victory for Jesus over both of these powerful men. And, characteristically enough, it is Luke alone who gives us the story of Jesus' encounter with the women of Jerusalem (23:27-28). It is also from Luke that we receive the tradition that Jesus' dying words were, not "Elohi, Elohi lamma sabacthani?" but "Father, into your hands I commend my spirit", not from Psalm 22 but from Psalm 31. So Luke portrays Jesus as the just Jewish martyr going to his fate, rather than the abandoned criminal that we saw in Mark's account.

This comes out most clearly, perhaps, in that wonderful episode which Luke inserts at 23:39-43, which reads as follows:

> *One of the crucified evildoers was blaspheming him saying:*
> *Are you not the Christ?*
> *Save yourself and us.*
>
> *But in answer the other reproached him saying:*
> *Do you not fear God, that you are under the same sentence?*
>
> *And we justly, for we are receiving a penalty that fits what we have done;*
> *whereas this man has done nothing out of place.*
>
> *And he said:*
> *Jesus, remember me when you come into your kingdom.*
>
> *And he said to him: Amen I say to you,*
> *TODAY with me you will be in Paradise.*

This is an unforgettable story, of course. It starts with Mark's version, except that for Mark both of those crucified with Jesus were reviling him. Here only one of them does that, and the other one fires up in Jesus' defence, exhorting his partner in strangely Lukan language to be a "God-fearer", and acquitting Jesus of any guilt: "this man has done nothing out of place". Then, having acquitted Jesus, he also promotes him to kingship: "Jesus, remember me when you come into your kingdom". What is most remarkable of all about this beautiful story is Jesus' reply, the hope resounding down the ages, and leaping off the page of the gospel into our era: "TODAY you will be with me in Paradise". I have printed the word "today" in capitals, because it is only sparingly used in Luke's gospel, and when it is used it is of considerable importance.

The first time it appears is at 2:11, when it is part of the angels' message to the shepherds. The next time we hear it is at 4:21, in that intensely dramatic episode which Luke places at the beginning of Jesus' ministry, in the synagogue at Nazareth, when he read that splendid text from Isaiah 61 ("the Spirit of the Lord is upon me, for he has anointed me to preach good news to the poor"), and concluded "TODAY this text is being fulfilled in your sight". The next time we hear it is in the reaction of the crowds on seeing the healing of a paralytic, at 5:26: "we have seen strange things TODAY". After that we encounter it again at 13:32-33, when it refers to Jesus continuing with his ministry and going calmly on towards his death. Then it appears twice in the story of Zacchaeus (19:5,9): "Zacchaeus, hurry on down, for TODAY I have to stay in your house" and "TODAY salvation has come to this house". The last use of it is at 22:34,61, referring to Jesus' prediction of the betrayal by Peter, and the fulfilment of that prediction.

So TODAY is in the time of the reader. Each of these uses of the word leaps from the page at us, demanding our instant response to the salvation that is on offer. As we have seen so often before in all the gospels, it is our story that is being spoken of here by the dying Jesus. But if we read it correctly there is enormous hope in the story; and we are left by Luke in no doubt that we are dealing with one who is really a king, making majestic arrangements for his subjects. At this moment the reader must decide which side he is on.

d) The Passion in John's Gospel

Once we reach the fourth gospel, the impression is chiefly one of the immense power of Jesus. This is dramatically expressed in John's account of the arrest in the garden, which reads as follows:

> *So Judas taking the cohort*
> *and helpers both from the high priests and from the Pharisees*
> *came there*
> *with torches and lamps and weapons.*
>
> *So Jesus knowing everything that was coming upon him*
> *went out and said to them:*
> *Whom do you seek?*

They replied to him:
Jesus the Nazarene.
He says to them:
EGO EIMI
And Judas the betrayer stood with them.

Therefore when he said to them:
EGO EIMI,
they went backwards and fell to the ground.

Therefore again he asked them:
Whom do you seek?
And they said:
Jesus the Nazarene.

Jesus replied :
I have said to you that EGO EIMI.
Therefore if you seek me,
let these go.

In order that the word might be fulfilled which he spoke:
Those whom you gave me, I have not lost any of them.

It is an extraordinary demonstration of Jesus' power, this episode as John presents it. Our eye is caught straightaway by the resources with which Judas evidently feels it necessary to surround himself: a cohort, which is to say a detachment of Roman soldiers, and helpers from the religious and intellectual establishments (High Priests and Pharisees). They come armed to the teeth, and, unlike Jesus, they need to bring "torches and lamps". Jesus, by contrast, relies only on his inner resources. He has no need, of course, of artificial lighting, for he has already been established in this gospel as "the light of the world".

The next thing we notice is that, not for the first time in this gospel, Jesus is in total command: "knowing everything that was coming upon him". And it is in keeping with this that it is Jesus, and not the arresting party, who conducts the interrogation: "whom do you seek?" They answer, obediently enough, "Jesus the Nazarene", to which he gives the powerful reply EGO EIMI. I have left that in the original Greek. Literally these words mean "I am" or "it is I"; but in John's gospel they appear frequently, as, for example in "before Abraham was, EGO EIMI"(8:58). To the attentive Jewish reader, however, the words will certainly have echoed God's encounter with Moses at Exodus 3, where Moses asks who he is speaking to and is given the sacred name I AM WHO I AM, or I AM (Exodus 3:14).

For reasons that are not wholly clear to us, the evangelist makes us notice that Judas has definitively aligned himself with the forces of darkness: "and Judas the betrayer stood with them". Not that it did "them" any good, as we now see the effect of this powerful title: "therefore [and we should puzzle about this word if we had the time] when he said to them EGO EIMI, they went backwards and fell to the ground". They cannot get away as easily as that however, but must submit to further interrogation: "whom do you seek?", to which they repeat the same answer as before.

And Jesus is unmistakably in charge, giving orders as to what they are to do: "I have said to you that EGO EIMI. Therefore if you seek me, let these go". The evangelist now adds a sentence indicating that this was to make Jesus' words come true, and that should make us stop and think, for it means that Jesus' words have now taken on the quality of Scripture, as sayings or prophecies that are verified after they have been spoken.

So there is a great deal of hope in the way John tells the story of Jesus' passion; here we are dealing with a Jesus who is wholly in charge. For another example of that look at the following passage:

> *Therefore the high priest interrogated Jesus*
> *about his disciples and about his teaching.*
>
> *Jesus replied to him:*
> *I have spoken openly to the world;*
> *I have always taught in synagogue and in the Temple,*
> *where all the Jews come together,*
> *and I have spoken nothing in secret.*
>
> *Why do you ask me?*
> *Ask those who heard what I said to them.*
> *See, these know what I said.*
>
> *As he was saying these things*
> *one standing by of the servants gave Jesus a slap saying,*
> *Do you answer thus the high priest?*
>
> *Jesus replied to him:*
> *If I have spoken badly, bear witness of the badness.*
> *But if well, why do you strike me?*
> *Therefore Annas sent him bound to Caiaphas the high priest.*

There are four different ways in this passage in which the evangelist emphasises Jesus' total control of the situation. Rather than my tediously pointing them all out to you, can I ask you to identify them? (Remember that there are very few "right answers" in Scripture scholarship, so the answers you reach here may easily be as good as mine).

You could read through the whole of the rest of the passion narrative in John's gospel to see how Jesus is presented as wholly in charge, going a royal road to his death. You might, for example, look at the long debate on kingship that takes up a full chapter, from 18:25 to 19:16, and count up the number of times Jesus or other people go "in" and "out"; and you might notice that the evangelist constructs two "stages" with these comings and goings, the outside one all noise and frenzy, and the inside one a quieter one, where the real debate is going on, between Jesus and the local representative of the greatest power on earth. There is no doubt at all who is in charge throughout the story.

So we are not surprised when Jesus is finally sentenced, to see him going out "carrying his cross for himself" (19:17); the Jesus of the other three gospels needed help to carry the cross, but in John Jesus is wholly in charge. Similarly, Pilate gives his final official verdict, in all three languages, that the accused is indeed "Jesus of Nazareth, the King of the Jews", and upholds his own verdict on appeal (19:19-22).

Even when Jesus is on the cross, it turns out to be a royal throne, by Pilate's official decree ("what I have written, I have written"); then, from this same throne, we find Jesus founding a dynasty: "woman, behold your son . . . behold your mother"(19:25-27). He remains, too, wholly in control to the very end: "after this, Jesus, knowing that all was already accomplished, thatthe Scripture might be fulfilled, said: I thirst" (19:28). There is no hint here of a dying agony, only a regal control over events. That is even clearer a few verses later when Jesus dies; here there is no sense of abandonment by God, as we had in Mark's gospel, but a gracious letting go of life: "Jesus said: it is accomplished, and bowing his head he gave up the ghost". That is majestic enough, but the phrase I have translated "gave up the ghost", or, as we might say, "expired", also means "handed over the Spirit". So our evangelist sees the cross as a place where royal favours are dispensed; and this sense is reinforced when the centurion puts the lance in Jesus' side, and out come blood and water, which for John's gospel certainly means the gift of the two sacraments known to the early Church, of baptism and eucharist. And, quite appropriately, Jesus is given a royal funeral (a hundred litres of oil, for Heaven's sake!) by two crypto-disciples who have emerged from the woodwork for the purpose (19:38-40).

So the evangelists give us four very different accounts of Jesus' passion; if however we find ourselves asking "but which is the *true* one?" we have missed the point of what a gospel is. We should be the poorer if we lacked any of these four stories, and less able to live in this country today. We need to tell ourselves this terrible story, to remind ourselves that ours is not the only society where people embrace the deceptively easy alternative of killing those one is in conflict with; it is important for us not to shirk the pain, so we need Mark's passion narrative, for instance. But, above all, we tell the story only because there is hope there, hope for us, and hope for all the hopeless ones who see nothing but violence menacing them. So if the versions offered by Matthew, Luke, and John reveal a progression away from the bleakness of Mark, that is not because they are trying to pretend that it was not nasty: it self-evidently was thoroughly nasty, this horrendously unjust death of Jesus. It is because gospel is about *now*, and we do not tell the fullness of the Jesus-story, which is our story, unless we allow it to talk, to those who have no hope, of the hope that is at the heart of the story.

Chapter 6

The Ambiguity of Resurrection

How do you read the Resurrection Stories in this country today?

Resurrection, at least according to St Paul, is at the centre of the Christian gospel, and it is impossible to read the Resurrection stories in the gospel without a lightening of the heart; but at the same time as the lifting of the heart there is often enough also a spinning of the head, because we find it all so hard to believe, and we mutter resentfully: "if *only* it were all true". I think that both the head-spinning and the heart-raising are detectable also in the gospel accounts of Jesus' resurrection, so we need not despair at our unbelief.

It may be helpful, before looking at some of the texts about what happened to Jesus after Good Friday, to make a few preliminary observations, which will underlie all that I shall say when discussing particular texts.

i) Resurrection can only be spoken of after crucifixion

Christians have always held resurrection and cross closely together, reflecting the profound insight of the gospels that the Resurrection is not any kind of *cheap* joy, but a costly one, which bears the scars of the suffering that went before. So, for example, the gospel of Luke (24:39-40) insists that the risen Jesus is also the Jesus that was wounded:

> "see my hands and my feet, that I am me; touch me and see,
> for a spirit does not have flesh and bones such as you see me having."
>
> And saying this he showed them the hands and the feet.

John's gospel makes the same point, only with greater directness (one might even call it crudity!), in chapter 20:20, 25, 27:

> *And saying this he showed them the hands and the side.*
> *So the disciples rejoiced, seeing the Lord . . .*
>
> *But [Thomas] said: if I do not see in his hands the mark of the nails*
> *and if I do not thrust my finger into the mark of the nails*
> *and if I do not thrust my hand into his side,*
> *I shall not believe . . .*
>
> *Then [Jesus] said to Thomas:*
> *bring your finger here and see my hands*
> *and bring your hand and thrust into my side,*
> *and don't be an unbeliever but a believer.*

Here, in other words, there is no faith in resurrection unless it is clearly established that the cross went before it. In South Africa at present (and in many other countries) we are looking for resurrection after a long nightmare of crucifixion, and as we read the gospel stories we can be cheered by their emphasis that there is no Easter without Good Friday.

ii) *Resurrection entails continuity with what went before*

This is related to our previous point. Resurrection, as the gospels understand it, is not resurrection if it does not bear the scars of crucifixion. It is not a magical wishing away of the awfulnesses of human life when it is exposed to radical evil; belief in resurrection entails the belief that even the worst awfulness can be taken up in the power of God. It does not involve the pretence that the awfulness never happened. We get some clues about this from the gospel stories of Resurrection. For example, in John 21, the character known as the beloved disciple comes to recognition of the mysterious person by the lakeside because he has worked a sign. After the remarkable and overwhelming catch of fish, we read in verse 7:

> *and so that disciple whom Jesus loved said to Peter:*
> *"it is the Lord".*

The mysterious person had done something that indicated that he was the one whom up to the crucifixion they had been accustomed to call "Lord". The same phenomenon is to be found in the touching account in John 20 of Mary Magdalene talking by the tomb with the one she thought to be the gardener. She does not know who it is until, as in the previous instance, the person does something familiar:

> *Jesus says to her: Mary.*
> *Turning, she says to him in Hebrew:*
> *Rabbouni (which means: teacher) (20:16).*

The moment of recognition comes when the tearful Mary hears a familiar form of address, which asserts that the person she is talking to is in continuity with the one who was previously known and loved. And Matthew's gospel preserves a slightly different version of the same event, at 28:9:

> *And, see, Jesus met the women saying: Hail [or: rejoice].*
> *And the women approached, and took hold of his feet, and worshipped him.*

Here we are left to assume that it is the familiar greeting, uttered in the well-known accent, that establishes the continuity of the one they meet with the one they knew before. The same is true of all our Easters. So, for example, the new will somehow emerge from the old in this country, and in all countries where resurrection is earnestly looked for; and the same is true of all our private crosses. The Lord does not take them away but uses them as part of the process of healing and reconstruction. How that is to be we can never really see when faced with the cross. It is only when we have passed through Good Friday into Easter Sunday that we can look back and see that it was so, and that our liberated joy is in continuity with the pain that previously oppressed us. If you want a clue as to how there could possibly be such a continuity, you might look at 1 Corinthians 15:35-49, where Paul, emphasising the centrality of resurrection to the gospel that he preached, compares it to the seed that is sown in the ground, which is both continuous and discontinuous with the plant that will eventually emerge.

iii) *Belief in Resurrection entails something more than the belief that Jesus is not dead.*

The gospels all understand the Resurrection of Jesus as something earth-shatteringly different from, for example, the raising of Lazarus in John 11. So in the original ending of John's gospel, in chapter 20, verse 28, when Thomas is invited to inspect the wounds that the Risen Jesus still bears, he does not say: "All right, I agree that it is Jesus", rather as a friend of Lazarus might have done. Instead, Thomas leaps way beyond the evidence that is before him, to make a very grand proclamation indeed, when he says "my Lord and my God". The title "Lord" is the one that Greek-speaking Jews had been accustomed to employ for the sacred name of God when they had occasion to translate it out of Hebrew, so it is a major one, and it is clear from the way in which this episode is presented, that the reader is meant to agree, as the gospel comes to its climax that Thomas has got it right. But what he has "got right" is something far bigger than what has previously been wrong.

That may be a helpful notion for people who find themselves asking: "what can God possibly do in this situation?" It is a perfectly sensible question, of course, because from our end it always seems impossible even to imagine anything that could possibly be done. In South Africa, as I write these words, we are very far from sure what things will be like after the elections; indeed, we are not even sure if there will be elections, nor who will compete in them if there are. And some people are fearful that a change of government might mean no more than a change of oppressors, when what we are looking for is really a new vision of what it means to live in society together. What we have to do therefore is to reflect on what God has *already* done. So we must look back to all that has happened since February 1990, when Nelson Mandela was released from prison, and be astonished at how things have already changed, in a country where injustice seemed set in concrete, and therefore take hope that things might yet change a great deal more. And while we do that with one hand, with the other we should be thumbing through the gospels, and see how Resurrection is more than just the resuscitation of Jesus, and therefore how a new South Africa could be much more than the old, written in black and white where once it was written in white and black. The gospel speaks, it cannot be too often emphasised, about our place and time, and only comes true when it is a story about our lives.

iv) Resurrection is "news too good to be true"

The fourth point is clearly related to several of the points we have already made. The fact is that it is desperately difficult to believe in the resurrection; people often find themselves saying "if only it could all be true". Well, in that respect we are not too different from our forebears in faith who passed down to us the resurrection stories. They knew how difficult it was to credit such a thing, whether in the life of Jesus or in our own lives: dead people, after all, do not commonly cease to be dead. So there is in the gospels a good deal of pointing to the empty tomb.

For example, in Mark's gospel, at 16:6, the young man whom the women rather unexpectedly find in Jesus' tomb, insists on the crude reality of the situation:

> *Don't be flabbergasted; you seek Jesus, the Nazarene, the crucified.*
> *He is not here; see the place where they laid him.*

This does not bring the women to Resurrection faith, but it does point to one severely practical element in that faith: the tomb was empty on that

Sunday morning. That does not *prove* the truth of this astonishingly good news, but it points in the right direction.

The same is true of what we find in Matthew's gospel, at 28:15. Matthew is the only evangelist who has the story of the guard mounted on the tomb, to prevent the disciples stealing the body; but on the Sunday morning the tomb was undeniably empty, and the soldiers have to be bribed to spread the story that the body had been stolen. But, of course,that story would have had no weight whatever, if it had been possible to point to a decomposing corpse that could be identified as that of Jesus of Nazareth.

The news is too good to be true, and it is neither astonishing nor shocking that people, even church people, from time to time find themselves scratching their heads and saying "it can't be so". We are dealing with the action of God, and God's action in our world is both more ordinary and more breathtaking than anything we can easily imagine. The empty tomb is a pointer, no more. It proves nothing, but acts as a reminder of past suffering, and leaves a question-mark hanging in the empty air. How that question-mark is to be coped with depends on the response of individual readers of the gospel, as they survey their own lives, and ask if the empty tomb points to something new and undreamt of, a "quantum leap" into God's new world. In this country today, faced with the possibility of liberation, we ask whether it might not turn out to be after all "news too good to be true". To our question the gospels respond by pointing at the empty tomb and asking us: does that suggest a way of expressing the "in-between" situation in which you find yourselves?

v) The Resurrection stories are remarkably brief and enigmatic

We have already said that according to Paul (1 Corinthians 15:1-2) the Resurrection is absolutely central to the preaching of the gospel. It may be worth reminding ourselves what he actually said:

> *Brothers and sisters, I am revealing to you*
> *the significance of the gospel which I gospelled to you,*
> *which you received, on which you are firmly positioned,*
> *and through which you are saved,*
> *in what terms I gospelled you, if you hold it fast,*
> *unless you made your faith commitment in vain.*

This is an amazingly long and solemn introduction to Paul's restatement of his original gospel, which has been described as a "gospel of four verbs", that Christ *died*, that he was *buried,* that he *rose on the third day*, and that he was *seen* by a large number of witnesses knew him well.

So for Paul, the earliest of our surviving writers in the NT, Resurrection is absolutely central. If you are not preaching the resurrection, then it is not the gospel that you are preaching. All the gospels end with the news that Christ is risen; and yet, compared with the Passion Narratives, the amount of space given by the evangelists to the Resurrection stories is astonishingly slight. Mark's gospel originally had only eight verses, before someone decided to add verses 9-20 in chapter 16. Matthew has just 20 verses, John originally had just 31, before chapter 21 was added, and Luke's is the longest account, with exactly 53 verses, but most of that (verses 13-35) is given over to just one story, the moving account of the walk to Emmaus, which we shall be looking at later. So the writers do not give much space to Resurrection; and not only that, but if you look at each of the resurrection stories, you will see that in each of them there is an enigmatic or ambiguous element: the participants in the story (and hence the reader) find themselves asking: "is it really true?" or indicating by what they do, for example running away from the tomb, that they are very far from sure that Jesus is risen.

This economy with regard to the Resurrection stories, and the hovering ambiguity that they engender seem to me quite apt; for our experience of Resurrection is never of the "knock-down" sort that *forces* you to believe. The Resurrection *is* "news too good to be true" and does not batter its way into our hearts, but gently invites and awaits our response. This point about the Resurrection narratives is obviously related to my final point.

vi) The reader needs to "step aboard" the Resurrection stories

One of the things that I have been arguing all the way through this book is that the gospels are incomplete until we accept the invitation to accept them into our lives, until we "step aboard" them, and make them our story. They are not, that is to say, intended to be stories about long ago, but stories that seduce us to make the gospel a part of our lives. And, of course, we shall never make them a part of our lives unless we choose to do so; we are not forced, for God never forces our hand, but says "come aboard if you will", or "try it and see".

The invitation is always open, however, and so the last half-sentence of Matthew's gospel is phrased in the *present* tense:

> and see, I am with you all the days, until the consummation of the world.
> (Mt 28:20).

The present tense leaps out of the pages of the gospel at us and demands a response. These words are no longer addressed to the "eleven" to whom the discourse is apparently addressed, but to anyone who picks up the gospel and makes it through until the end. The Risen Lord offers his presence but does not obtrude it, for love cannot be compelled and is the enemy of force.

vii) *Two Resurrection Stories* :

a) A Very Odd Ending (Mark 16:1-8):

With these observations in mind, let us look at two of the Resurrection stories. The first, you may think, is not really a Resurrection story at all, for it does not (apparently) recount an appearance of Jesus to those who knew him before his death. It is the story with which Mark originally ended his gospel, and reads as follows:

> *And when the Sabbath had dragged by,*
> *Mary the Magdalene, and Mary of James and Salome*
> *bought spices so that they might go and anoint him.*
>
> *And very very early on day one of the sabbaths*
> *they come to the tomb;*
> *but the sun had risen.*
>
> *And they were saying to themselves:*
> *Who will roll away the stone for us from the gate of the tomb?*
>
> *And looking up they see that the stone has been rolled away,*
> *for it was very large.*
>
> *And going into the tomb they saw*
> *a young man sitting on the right wearing a white robe.*
> *And they were thunderstruck.*
>
> *But he says to them:*
> *do not be thunderstruck:*
> *you seek Jesus, the Nazarene, the one that was crucified.*
> *He is risen, he is not here.*
> *See the place where they laid him.*
>
> *But go, tell his disciples*
> *and Peter:*
> *He is going before you into Galilee - there you will see him,*
> *as he told you.*
>
> *And the women going out fled from the tomb,*
> *for they were held by fear and astonishment.*
> *And they said nothing to nobody,*
> *for they were afraid . . .*

It is a remarkable story this (how often I have said that in the course of this book!) with which Mark opted to end his gospel. Now you may be irritably wondering if I am going to prove that assertion. Well I am not, for you can never really prove things in the world of Scripture scholarship; but you might care to consider the following facts: firstly, many manuscripts end where my translation ends, at verse 8, with the women running away and saying nothing to anyone. Secondly, there are in the manuscript tradition two other endings to Mark, the "long ending", which is verses 9-20, and is very largely a meditation on other post-resurrection stories, and the "short ending". Thirdly, neither the "long ending" nor the "short ending" sounds like the way Mark normally writes. So it is a fair bet that Mark originally ended his gospel at verse 8 of chapter 16, and at least two other people found that an unsatisfactory ending, either because there is no account of a Resurrection appearance of Jesus, or because they did not care for the women's fear as an appropriate ending for a gospel. Mark, I suppose, might have muttered that since he *invented* the gospel form, he might be expected to know what makes a suitable ending for it.

No more on that; let us look at how Mark tells the story:

> And when the Sabbath had dragged by,
> Mary the Magdalene, and Mary of James and Salome
> bought spices so that they might go and anoint him.

This is, as a matter of fact, the last normal verse in the whole gospel. I have tried to convey in my translation the idea that is there in the Greek, of the long drawn-out Sabbath. We notice that the protagonists of the story are women, which is striking enough. We notice further that they were going to do a woman's job, of anointing the corpse, and that at this stage they did not believe in the Resurrection. For of course you only anoint bodies that are safely dead (with the brave exception of the unnamed woman in Mark 14:3-9, which may be connected somehow with our story).

> And very very early on day one of the sabbaths
> they come to the tomb;
> but the sun had risen.

Mark is always very sparing in his indications of time, and one always has the feeling that they actually mean something, even when it does not seem possible to establish what that something is. What occurs to me is that when Mark says "on day one of the sabbaths", he may be dropping the reader a broad hint that this is a very new beginning. Certainly he is insistent on the earliness of the hour when they come to the tomb, though that seems slightly at odds with his noting that "the sun had risen", and I have often wondered whether this might not be a little joke at the women's expense. And if male readers are tempted into affixing a superior smirk to their patriarchal lips, they might just ask themselves where the men disciples are at this precise moment.

> *And they were saying to themselves:*
> *Who will roll away the stone for us from the gate of the tomb?*

Once again, it is no good us saying "you should have thought of the stone before you set out". For at least they set out and went to the tomb, that dwelling-place of demons, while the men could not be seen for dust. But there is a further point here, and that is that Resurrection is a matter of God effortlessly rolling away all our stones.

> *And looking up they see that the stone has been rolled away,*
> *for it was very large.*

Mark uses words very carefully, and the word that I have translated "looking up" is not often used in this gospel. We meet it at 6:41 and 7:34, where it describes Jesus, just before he performs a miracle. But the other three times where it is used, at 8:24, and 10:51,52, it actually means "seeing again", and it may be that this is what we are to understand here: the women are given new sight.

And what about the mysterious comment: "for it was very large"? Some scholars, dull fellows, have suggested that it really belongs with the previous verse, when they were wondering aloud about how the stone was to be rolled away. But what Mark is doing is persuading us to gasp at the power of God to roll away all the stones in the lives of those who read the gospel.

> *And going into the tomb they saw*
> *a young man sitting on the right wearing a white robe.*
> *And they were thunderstruck.*

Now this is a brave gesture on the part of the women, for it would have been seen as playing with fire, actually to go into a tomb, even if the sun "had risen", since that was where demons lurked. And they are rewarded for their bravery with a mysterious encounter, the first of many in the Resurrection narratives. It is with a "young man", whom Mark does not trouble to identify.

Who was this young man? We think inevitably of the young man who had run away naked at 14:51, and reflect that he had left behind a "shroud", rather as Jesus may be presumed to have done. But there Mark used a slightly different Greek word; and inevitably the reader is puzzled. We also notice that the young man is "sitting on the right"; and the last time we heard that phrase, it was on the lips of Jesus, at his trial (14:62), when he quoted Psalm 110: "you will see the Son of Man sitting on the right". So inevitably the reader starts to wonder if the young man is meant to be Jesus, particularly as he is seen to be "wearing a white robe", which inevitably reminds us of the transfiguration (9:3), where the wording was a bit different, but the effect very much the same. Lastly, the women are "thunderstruck", a word that in Mark's gospel often refers to the effect of Jesus' teaching or actions. So as we listen to what the young man has to say, a question-mark is forming in our minds: are these brave women in fact talking to the risen Jesus, without recognising him as such?

> *But he says to them:*
> *do not be thunderstruck:*
> *you seek Jesus, the Nazarene, the one that was crucified.*
> *He is risen, he is not here.*
> *See the place where they laid him.*

Like Jesus (e.g. 6:50), he tells the women not to be thunderstruck; and he shows a remarkable knowledge of their situation: he knows who they are looking for. Then for the first time in this episode, the good news is proclaimed: "he is risen". And that is immediately followed by a line that would seem to eliminate any possibility that it might be Jesus to whom they are talking, for the young man says "he is not here", which would obviously not be true if the young man *were* Jesus. But that may be too drearily literal a way of reading the text, and we must perhaps allow the question-mark to remain hanging in the air. The young man is, after all, only referring to the fact that the corpse they expected is not there: "see the place where they laid him", and is not necessarily denying or concealing that *he* is the one who was dead and is risen.

At all events, the young man is a personage of sufficient status to be able to give them orders:

> *But go, tell his disciples*
> *and Peter:*
> *He is going before you into Galilee - there you will see him,*
> *as he told you.*

And very remarkable orders they are too. In the first place, we note that the women are being made apostles to the apostles, that it is they to whom the good news about Resurrection is entrusted, to pass it on, along with some implicit instructions. Secondly, we find ourselves asking where the disciples are: the last time we saw them they were making a good pace in the opposite direction (14:50). Thirdly, Peter is singled out for special mention here; Peter, whom we saw not long ago cursing and swearing the most terrible oaths that he had never heard of Jesus, is now mentioned by name. Fourthly, the men are to see Jesus not in Jerusalem, but in "Galilee", which is probably to be understood as "Galilee of the Gentiles", that is to say, wherever the lonely and disappointed Christians of Mark's church find themselves preaching the gospel, the risen Jesus will be there with them. And the word that I have translated "he is going before you" could also mean "he is leading you". That may be important, for, fifthly, the men do not have very much to rely on by way of proof here, except that Jesus said it would be so. The disciple has to find the risen Lord by preaching about him in a world that does not seem very interested in such stories. Lastly, the verse ends "as he told you", and we find ourselves asking who "you" are. It could be the male disciples, or it could be the women; but all the time we need to remember that the gospel is our story, and that these words are in fact addressed to us who read the gospel.

Next we come to the words with which Mark's gospel originally ended:

> *And the women going out fled from the tomb,*
> *for they were held by fear and astonishment.*
> *And they said nothing to nobody,*
> *for they were afraid . . .*

To get the full effect of these words, imagine yourself sitting in the house where Mark's church met, and listening to him go through the whole story, and hearing that verse, and suddenly realising that he is rolling up the scroll and putting it away, and that there is no more gospel to come. Do you not find yourself standing on your seat and objecting: "but they *must* have said something to somebody; otherwise we should not be here!"? Mark intends us to be shocked by this extraordinary turn of events, which is no more extraordinary in itself than the whole gospel has been from the beginning (and I wish that I had space and time to share with you just what an extraordinary thing Mark's gospel really is).

Consider what we have just heard; that the women have been given the exciting news about resurrection. That is of itself something of a shock, for Mark's readers would probably not have been accustomed to considering women as reliable witnesses. Then, just like the swineherds at Gadara (5:14) and the disciples at Gethsemane(14:50), and the naked young man (14:52), they flee. Mark gives a reason for this precipitate flight: "because *trembling* and *astonishment* held them". Now these are very Marcan words. The woman with the flow of blood (5:33) also trembled, while the word for astonishment is applied to the following groups of people: the witnesses to the raising to life of the 12 year-old girl (5:42), the witnesses to the cure of the paralytic (2:12), and those in the boat after the walking on the water (6:51), as they tried to work out what it all meant. There is one other use of the verb, when it is applied to Jesus, by his family, who thought he was crazy, but that probably does not help us to understand what is going on here. The point is that it is often the reaction to an encounter with the truth about Jesus; so Mark is dropping us a broad hint that the women have grasped the awe-inspiring truth. That being the case, Mark is certainly not telling us to take seriously his apparent claim that the women did not fulfil their commission. Something else is going on here, which we have had occasion to refer to at other places in this book. What is happening is that we, the reader, are being invited to "step aboard" at this point, and to take seriously our responsibilities in the matter of the spreading of the gospel. It is an awe-inspiring and tremble-making message, the news that the dying Messiah is risen, but the gospel does not become gospel until the reader preaches it and lives it. So the ending "and to nobody said nothing because they were afraid" is not an ending but only a beginning.

b) The Walk to Emmaus (Luke 24:13-35)

This story is deservedly loved by a good many people above all the Resurrection narratives. I am going to suggest that this is because it openly invites us to "step aboard", and that it is in fact a "liturgy of word and bread", which any disappointed Christians may attend. First, let us read the story, as though for the first time. It goes something like this:

And see two of them on the day itself
were journeying to a village 60 stades away from Jerusalem,
whose name was Emmaus,
and they were talking to each other
about all these things that had happened.

And it happened as they chatted and debated, and Jesus himself drew near
and was journeying with them.

But their eyes were held so as not to recognise him.

And he said to them:
what are these words which you throw at each other as you walk?
And they stood still, looking sullen.

And one of them answered, Cleopas by name, and he said to him:
Are you the only stranger in Jerusalem that you do not know
the things that happened in her in these days?

And he said to them: what things?
And they said to him: the things about Jesus the Nazarene,
who was a man, a prophet,
powerful in deed and word before God and before all the people,

and how they handed him over, our high priests and our rulers,
to a judgement of death, and they crucified him.

But we had expected that he was the one who was going to redeem Israel.
And now with all this he is spending this third day
since these things happened.

BUT some women from us have amazed us:
turning up early at the tomb,

and not finding his body they came saying that they had also seen a vision
of angels, who say he is alive.

And some of those with us went off to the tomb,
and they found it just exactly like the women said;
but him they did not see.

And HE said to them:
O foolish and slow of heart to believe in all the things
that the prophets said.

Was it not inevitable that the Messiah should suffer these things
and enter into his glory?

And beginning from Moses and from all the prophets
he interpreted to them in all the Scriptures
the things about himself.

And they drew near to the village to which they were journeying,
and he pretended that he was journeying further.

And they prevailed upon him saying:
Stay with us, because it is towards evening,
and the day has gone to bed.
And he went in to stay with them.

And it happened when he lay down with them to eat,
taking bread he blessed, and breaking gave to them.

And their eyes were opened and they recognised him,
and he became invisible to them.

And they said to each other: was not our heart burning
when he spoke to us on the way
when he opened to us the scriptures?

And rising up at that very hour
they returned to Jerusalem, and they found gathered together
the twelve and those with them,

saying that in fact the Lord is risen
and has appeared to Simon.

And they expounded to them the things on the way
and how he was known to them in the breaking of the bread.

It is a wonderful story this, but it is important not to lose sight of the fact that it is unmistakably about the present day. It describes a liturgy, such as Christians have celebrated ever since that first Easter Sunday, finding the Risen Lord to be present at the breaking of the bread.

And see two of them on the day itself
were journeying to a village 60 stades away from Jerusalem,
whose name was Emmaus.

Already our curiosity is aroused, for we wonder who the "them" are of whom two are reported to be making this journey. There is nothing in what precedes to indicate who it might be, so we simply assume it to be any two disciples, who might be identical with any two readers of the gospel. The distance of the journey, and the name of the village to which they were heading, are presumably both irrelevant, and should be understood as referring to any disciple's journey and any destination. And Luke allows us to eavesdrop on what they are saying:

and they were talking to each other about all these things
that had happened.

And it happened as they chatted and debated,
and Jesus himself drew near and was journeying with them.

But their eyes were held so as not to recognise him.

This is surely Luke painting one of his memorable pictures. Here the picture includes the problems of present-day disciples, but also carries their solution; for they are deeply absorbed in their problems: "all these things that had happened", as we frequently are absorbed in our own misery. Luke tells us, however, that we do not walk alone, for he lets us know, what the two disciples do not yet know, that Jesus is walking with them; and we are to reflect on our own situation, where Jesus seems either absent or impenetrably disguised, and let light slowly dawn.

And he said to them:
what are these words which you throw at each other as you walk?
And they stood still, looking sullen.

Now, I suggest, the liturgy is about to start, as always, with the Lord's initiative and invitation. Jesus asks them a question, which is directed to us too, and it turns them into sulky adolescents. The point here is that both Jesus and the liturgy always start where we are, not waiting for us to get to where we "ought" to be.

And one of them answered, Cleopas by name, and he said to him:
Are you the only stranger in Jerusalem that you do not know
the things that happened in her in these days?

We do not know who Cleopas might have been, but he can stand for anyone who feels cheated in their faith in Jesus, or senses, as many people do in this country today, that "God has abandoned us". He now turns his aggression on the newcomer who is asking impertinent and uninvited questions, and responds with a question of his own. But, of course, there is a perfectly splendid irony here, for the "stranger" whom he berates is not a stranger at all, but the Jesus whom they are looking for; and so far from being the only one in Jerusalem who does not know what has happened recently, is actually the only person who *does* know.

And he said to them: what things?
And they said to him: the things about Jesus the Nazarene,
who was a man, a prophet,
powerful in deed and word before God and before all the people,

and how they handed him over, our high priests and our rulers,
to a judgement of death, and they crucified him.

Now starts that part of the liturgy known as the Penitential Rite, in which the worshippers are invited to state before the Lord where they are "at". Jesus sets the process going with a question, like a skilled teacher, and they share their disappointments and sense of alienation. First, they report the facts about Jesus, with a certain amount of interpretation, when they identify Jesus as not merely a man, but also "a prophet, powerful in word and deed before God and all the people". The language here is the language of Luke: see a similar example at Acts 7:22, and, for God described as "the powerful one", Luke 1:49.

Next they describe the extent of the catastrophe that has hit them : "they handed him over, our establishment . . . and crucified him". Cleopas has decided that this is the end of the Jesus-story, as human beings often decide that a particular story has come to an end, where from God's point of view it is only beginning. So there is great sadness here, as there often is at the start of a liturgy when people bring their batteredness and weariness. And the sadness continues in Cleopas' next words:

But we had expected that he was the one who was going to redeem Israel.
And now with all this he is spending this third day since these things
happened.

There is a very profound sense here of being let down by God, that many Christians have experienced; but of course the reader has already been told that it is in fact Jesus to whom Cleopas is pouring out his woes, and therefore sees quite another perspective on it; we know, because Luke has told us, that they were right who supposed that Jesus "was the one who was going to redeem Israel". And we are confirmed in this reading when we hear Cleopas speak of the "third day"; for we have heard this phrase twice only in the gospel so far, and on each occasion it was when Jesus predicted his sufferings (9:22; 18:33). Now if it was predicted, then it is less of a meaningless catastrophe, for prediction gives control and therefore meaning; but in any case, on both occasions the "third day" was the day on which, after all the sufferings, the Son of Man was to be "raised up". So there is hope here, after all, even if the men are slow to recognise it.

> *BUT some women from us have amazed us:*
> *turning up early at the tomb,*
>
> *and not finding his body they came saying that they had also seen a vision*
> *of angels, who say he is alive.*
>
> *And some of those with us went off to the tomb,*
> *and they found it just exactly like the women said;*
> *but him they did not see.*

I have printed the "but" with which these words start in capitals, for it is a curiously emphatic, and characteristically Lucan, phrase that is used here. It is meant to be a very large "but", reminding us that Cleopas and the other males had at their disposition such evidence about Jesus' resurrection as was available, but had not given it its proper weight. The fact is that evidence that would pass in a court of law is not the kind of thing that leads to faith in Resurrection. We notice, first, the implied contempt for women's testimony, and the total lack of admiration for their courage; secondly, the women had sufficient evidence: an empty tomb, and a vision of angels. Now to the experienced Bible reader, that means that it is true, for that is how Biblical angels function (unlike dreams in Homer, for example). But, of course, in a court of law, an empty tomb proves nothing, and spiritual sightings prove even less. Resurrection is a tantalisingly ambiguous experience; as we read the story we know it to be true, but when our lives take the kind of turn that Cleopas' has we are not half so sure.

The men were evidently interested enough to check out the tomb; and what they saw confirmed the women's claims. The tomb was empty enough, but "him they did not see". This is hardly surprising if the tomb was empty, of course; but it carries a subtle hint of their unrequited longing to see the risen Jesus.

At this point we start what may be called the "liturgy of the word", when the Bible is read, and a homily delivered, in which the mysterious stranger takes up their experience, and relates it to Scripture (what we are trying, however inadequately, to do in this book):

> *And HE said to them:*
> *O foolish and slow of heart to believe in all the things*
> *that the prophets said.*
>
> *Was it not inevitable that the Messiah should suffer these things and enter into his glory?*
>
> *And beginning from Moses and from all the prophets he interpreted to them in all the Scriptures the things about himself.*

Luke introduces the sermon with a curiously emphatic Greek expression, which I have tried to convey by translating "and HE", meaning by that "the one they were longing for and did not realise they were talking to, and the one you, the reader, have often longed for, and who was always present, in his obscure way". The sermon starts, as sermons too often start, with a re-proach "O foolish and slow of heart"; but the message is very far from reproachful, and climaxes with the implicit affirmation of what human beings most want to know, that God, despite all the available evidence, really is in charge, and that acts of violence and feelings of lonely misery are not the whole story of the human plight. If it was truly "inevitable" that the Messiah should suffer in this way, then it is possible that Jesus was after all this Messiah, and that God has some idea, after all, of how to run the universe.

Next we are plunged back into the reader's own world, for the two men arrive at the destination for which they had set out from Jerusalem, several weary hours ago; but it seems curiously incomplete:

> *And they drew near to the village to which they were journeying,*
> *and he pretended that he was journeying further.*

They have arrived, but are now conscious that they need something more:

> *And they prevailed upon him saying:*
> *Stay with us, because it is towards evening,*
> *and the day has gone to bed.*
> *And he went in to stay with them*

We remember that when this conversation first started it was Jesus who initiated it; now the sermon has cast its spell, and they want more of the same. The day is virtually at an end, runs the excuse; but we see that what they are after is in fact the permanent presence of Jesus: "stay with us" has the same ambiguity in Greek as it does in English, so that it could mean either "spend the night" or "never leave us". It is the reaction of every believer on whom faith in the Resurrection has started to dawn. Although it is our *own* experience that we are watching unfold, we know that it is Jesus whom they are addressing, and who *pretends* to go on, before being restrained by the prayer of these post-Easter Christians.

So he accepts their invitation to be a permanent presence with them, and now he is in charge again, and we are quite clearly into the eucharistic liturgy:

> *And it happened when he lay down with them to eat,*
> *taking bread he blessed, and breaking gave to them.*

None of Luke's first readers could have missed the significance of the gesture, as Jesus presides at his own post-Resurrection liturgy. Luke had used virtually the same words at the Last Supper (22:19), and exactly the same words at the feeding of the 5,000 (9:16), where they were also "lying down". And, we may presume, those first Christians heard those words and watched the presider perform the same action each time they met for the eucharist.

However the eucharist is not a magical ceremony; it is not enough for Jesus or the presider merely to break and bless, for some response is required also from those who are present, and this liturgy is no exception:

> *And their eyes were opened and they recognised him,*
> *and he became invisible to them.*

That moment of revelation, the discovery that the risen Jesus is after all present with Christians who break bread is the reason why it has been repeated over and over again since there was a Christianity. And familiar, too, is the discovery of the "disappearing Jesus"; just when you think you have him taped or trapped or safe in a box, he "becomes invisible". But because of the liturgy they have been through, and the homily they have heard, it no longer matters to them that Jesus is absent again, whereas at the beginning of the journey it mattered quite terribly:

> *And they said to each other: was not our heart burning*
> *when he spoke to us on the way*
> *when he opened to us the scriptures?*

Now they do what all Christians must learn to do, and reflect on their experience of Jesus, talking to each other about it, the experience that is "on the way", that is to say in our daily life, and the experience that comes from prayerful reading of the Bible, "when he opened to usthe Scriptures". This book is really trying to bring both those essential elements together, of experience and Bible-reading, to find God in that experience.

Of course, this experience of God is not a private affair, that we can keep to ourselves; and a liturgy that simply leaves us thinking "what a wonderful experience" has not yet done its job. It remains incomplete, just as a gospel remains incomplete, until we find ourselves stimulated by it into action. This is what now happens to these newly-enthused disciples:

> *And rising up at that very hour*
> *they returned to Jerusalem, and they found gathered together*
> *the twelve and those with them,*
>
> *saying that in fact the Lord is risen*
> *and has appeared to Simon.*
>
> *And they expounded to them the things on the way*
> *and how he was known to them in the breaking of the bread.*

Luke is a deft word-painter. Remember how long and weary the journey was when the two set out for Emmaus; and how when they got there it was so late that there was no point in Jesus going any further. Now ask yourself how long the journey back to Jerusalem takes. The answer is "about a second-and-a-half", and it certainly stands as the Holy Land record for the distance. That is what good liturgy does: it gives us the presence of Jesus, which enables us to do the impossible, and to preach to others.

So they return to Jerusalem, and do something that all Christians must do; they share their experience of Jesus. This enables others to confirm that experience and be confirmed. So the "twelve and those with them" confirm this tale of resurrection (for it must always be the Church that confirms the worth of our own private experiences of Jesus), while the two men in return "expounded the things on the way", where the "way" represents the Christian journey through life, with all its miseries, which eventually find their meaning "in the breaking of the bread".

viii) Conclusion

What are we to make of all this? How are we to read the accounts in our circumstances today? Firstly, that we are not here speaking of "opium of the people" or "pie in the sky by and by when you die", to use the contemptuous phrases that are sometimes employed to dismiss talk of Resurrection. If Resurrection means anything at all, if liturgy is not to be a palliative, they must face squarely the actual situation in which people are living, and in those situations, which sometimes seem impossible and irremediable, offer hope to the hopeless. Resurrection-stories are about this country now, or they are about nothing at all. Christianity certainly involves belief in a life after death, for it involves the affirmation that God is nursing the human project and reluctant to let it die; but that does not mean, and cannot ever mean, that we can ignore the life before death, for it is in that life that we are called to walk with the Risen Jesus, and with those who do not yet believe, or who simply cannot believe, that Jesus could possibly be risen, or that there is a God in charge of this universe.

Chapter 7

Women in the New Testament

The question of the rights of women is one that is receiving urgent attention today; and in South Africa it has been linked with the denial of rights that the doctrine of *apartheid* implied. It seemed therefore a fruitful topic to consider while examining the question of "setting the gospel free"; for there are many feminist critics who would argue that Christianity is irredeemably biased against women, and must be jettisoned if women's rights are ever to be respected. While I think that view is too strongly expressed, it contains a germ of truth, and needs to be taken seriously if we are trying to argue that the gospel is an instrument of God's liberation of the human race. What I should like to do in this chapter is look at some New Testament texts that may offer some help on the question of women, and examine some that seem to relegate women to second-class status, to see what we can do with them, short of pretending that they do not actually exist.

i) Preliminary remarks

a) The question is an urgent one today

This is not a question that is going to disappear, if only we can bury our heads in the sand for long enough. I have been startled to discover how much pain Anglican friends of mine in England have been experiencing at the prospect, and now at the fact, of the ordination of women as priests; and while I do not wish that pain on them, and think it must be taken seriously, I am certain that they are swimming against an irresistible tide. And if a tide is *irresistible*, then it is of God, and not to be resisted. Other churches have long had women ministers, and look in astonishment at the ructions within the Anglican communion and the defensive responses of certain Catholic observers. There is also in our day a renewed awareness of the equality, and therefore of the equal rights, of all human beings. That is not to say that one should ride rough-shod over all the objections to the ordination of women. Some of these, admittedly, are frivolous, or scanty veilings of naked prejudice; but many are weighty and need to be given serious attention. What we cannot do is wait for the storm to pass. There is an issue here that all Christians, even from those groups who have already women in positions of leadership, need to face. Women are, after all, the majority among Christians, and any refusal to allow a structural openness for women's gifts will mean a terrible impoverishment for Christianity.

b) The question is bedevilled by deeply-held prejudices

When we discuss questions of this sort, very profound emotions can be stirred up. There is nothing wrong with this, provided that we are aware what is happening. Therefore men in particular must be aware if their blood-pressure starts to rise, and if we find ourselves getting irritable in the face of feminist criticism of male dominance of Church structures. This irritation can reveal to us our hidden assumptions of which we may not be aware, the assumption, for example, that women are inferior and need to be governed by us. We may have such a prejudice, and shrink from expressing it, and even only become aware of it when we find ourselves reacting irrationally against feminist arguments. Sometimes these unthought reactions present themselves to us in more acceptable guises. For example, we may find ourselves saying "I'm so *bored* with this question". That can be a defence mechanism against pressure that we do not really know how to resist. Or we find ourselves muttering "they are so strident". In this case we might be talking about militant feminists, but it is an adjective we might use for any "they" who threaten to upset our equilibrium. Or, again, we might say, to ourselves, or to safe male cronies "they are all so hideous". This could carry several meanings: it might mean "all feminism is unfeminine", or, more unpleasantly, the implication might be "they would not agitate for women's rights if they were attractive enough and could find a husband or boyfriend". Either way, this reaction is a way of saying to ourselves "I don't have to face this issue". But we do have to face it, for it seems that it may be a challenge to us from God. So while our defence mechanisms are important and must be listened to, they are not the final court of appeal, and must not be used to resist the gentle but firm challenge that Scripture offers us.

c) The Bible is patriarchal and androcentric

The Bible, so far as we know, was written almost entirely by men. Inevitably, therefore, it is "androcentric", that is to say, written from a male point of view. It is also "patriarchal". That means that it assumes, and therefore implicitly commends, a view of society as largely hierarchical, with father in charge, and women and children submissive, if they know their place, to the patriarch's authority. To say that is not, at least not as far as I am concerned, a criticism of the Scriptures as such. For the authors of Holy Writ were all men (or perhaps a few women) of their time and place, with all the prejudices of their contemporaries and fellow-tribesmen, just as this book is an inevitable reflection of the prejudices of an Englishman of a certain kind. "Aha!", you riposte, "but then you are not inspired, whereas Christians hold that the scriptural writers were". Very true, but whatever we mean by inspiration does not include the view that the evangelists, for example, ceased to be human, with a human's prejudices and errors. All biblical writers will have held, like Jesus himself, that the sun goes round the earth, which we now know not to be true. That does not mean that what they wrote was not the authoritative expression of the Word of God for Jewish and Christian believers.

Given, then, that the Bible is patriarchal and androcentric, we cannot deny that it has been used to justify the exploitation of women. We may wish to argue that that is not the *intention* of the biblical authors (though in some cases one wonders); we cannot deny that certain texts have been used to keep women in their place, and that place a suitably inferior one. Now, if such exploitation is not the will of God, then we need to read the Bible in such a way as to filter out the irrelevant or dangerous cultural presuppositions of its authors, to apply what is nowadays called a "hermeneutics of suspicion". There is nothing terribly tricky about this: a "hermeneutics of suspicion" is what you apply when listening to a politician, or a television announcer, or a schoolboy denying a misdemeanour, whom you think may be pulling a fast one. What you are trying to do is consciously to make allowance for a perceived prejudice.

Therefore when we read the Bible, what we have to do in this area is "look for the women", and ask where they have got to, or who is representing their point of view. For example, it is clear from the Resurrection narratives that Mary Magdalen was appointed the "apostle to the apostles", who preached to them the good news that Jesus was risen; yet she does not appear in the Acts of the Apostles, which is ostensibly the history of the young church. Another part of this "hermeneutics of suspicion" is looking out for vigorous polemic against females who get above themselves; that is a sure sign of a lively feminist movement. So one of the things we have to do is "read between the lines" of our Bibles.

d) Christianity is, or should be, profoundly egalitarian

There is no room in the Christianity presented to us by our earliest documents for a "hierarchy" in which some people are more "important" than others. Therefore many feminist readers of the Bible are today critical of its "patriarchalism", for even *benevolent* patriarchy fails to acknowledge the fundamental equality of the people of God that the New Testament asserts.

In connection with this, it may be necessary to use "she" occasionally for God, as a counter-witness to the all-pervasive male pronoun, and to avoid the use of "man" and "he" when we mean human beings in general. Many people find the female personal pronoun distressing in this context, but it might be quite important for them to try and get in touch with the source of their distress. It may not be so much a profound theological insight as an ungrounded prejudice that is operating here, and if that is the case, then we are better off without it. God is no more "he" than God is "she"; we have in Christianity an intensely personal sense of God, whom Jesus addressed intimately as "abba", and something in us therefore revolts against calling God by the neuter pronoun "it". In Hebrew, Greek, and Latin, God (as opposed to goddesses) is masculine; and for the Hebrew scriptures, from whom we get much of our talk about God, it would have been particularly difficult, though grammatically possible, to speak of God as "she", because of the existence of Canaanite goddesses to whom YHWH might have been assimilated. And if a reader particularly versed in Aramaic is disposed to point out that "Abba" means father, and is therefore indisputably male, I should have to reply that the intimacy of this absolute form in Aramaic is such that it might better be translated "Father and Mother", or "Daddy and Mummy", except that there is, of course, only one God, for us as for Jesus.

God is therefore neither "he" nor "she"; but in English we have to use one or the other very often, or be led into clumsy circumlocutions. Therefore it seems to me that we need to innure ourselves to the unfamiliar "God Herself", if we are to do justice to the reality about God. Nor is it a remote and academic matter; the growing awareness of the rights of women means that we must stoutly resist anything that tends to deny the equality of the sexes (even by way of placing women on the safety of a pedestal!). And there is a subtle (because never stated in this way) argument that runs as follows: since God is male, therefore male is superior to female, and just as God the Father runs the universe, so the father, or patriarch, runs the family, and must be obeyed in all things, and women and children are inferior. From which it follows that men alone are permitted to have power in the church. It will become clear in what follows (it is doubtless already clear) that I do not believe that this view does full justice to the teaching of the New Testament. For one thing, and this is something on which we must listen most attentively to feminist exegetes, Jesus is quite clear that his disciples are not to play the power game, which is a trap into which males can all too easily fall.

What I should like to do in the rest of this chapter is very simple. First, we shall look at a text which I shall argue is very revealing of Jesus' attitude to women. Secondly, since many observers are inclined to blame St Paul for what they regard as the Church's benighted attitude to the question, we shall examine the relevant Pauline texts.

ii) *Jesus and a Woman: Mark 5: 24-34*

The text that we shall read together is the following beautiful story:

> *And a great crowd was following him,*
> *and they pressed in upon him.*
>
> *And a woman who had had a flow of blood for twelve years*
>
> *and had suffered much from many doctors*
> *and had spent all she had*
> *and had not been helped by it, but rather she had got worse,*
>
> *hearing about Jesus,*
> *coming in the crowd behind him,*
> *touched his garment.*
>
> *For she said: If I just touch his garments,*
> *I shall be saved.*
>
> *And immediately the fountain of her blood was dried up*
> *and she knew in her body*
> *that she was healed of her suffering.*
>
> *And immediately Jesus knowing in himself*
> *the power going out of him,*
> *turning round in the crowd said:*
> *who touched my garments?*
>
> *And his disciples said:*
> *do you see the crowd pressing upon you, and you say:*
> *who touched me?*
>
> *And he looked round to see the woman who had done this.*
>
> *And the woman in fear and trembling*
> *knowing what had happened to her*
> *came and fell before him and told him all the truth.*
>
> *And he said to her:*
> *daughter, your faith has saved you.*
> *Go in peace, and be clean of your suffering.*

Mark's attitude to women is very interesting, and very sensitive. You might reflect on the unnamed woman who anoints Jesus at the beginning of the passion narrative, who appears as a *true* disciple, or Simon's mother-in-law, who ministered to Jesus after she had been cured, and so proved herself a disciple in the Jesus tradition (1:31), or the Syro-Phoenician woman in chapter 7, the only person ever to make Jesus change his mind, or those brave women who are discovered watching from afar off at the crucifixion(15:41). I think that Mark offers his women as role-models of what disciples should be like; whether or not that is so, this story fits well into the pattern. It is a lovely story, and one that you feel could hardly be invented, so it tells us a good deal about Jesus, as well as about Mark.

There is another feature about this story that we should notice before we examine it in greater detail; it is a technique that Mark often employs, which I call "sandwiching". A grander title, if you go in for grand titles, might be "interpretative interweaving". What Mark does is to wrap one story round another story, so that the reader is forced, or at least encouraged, to take the two together, and read them as shedding light each on the other. Two good examples of that (and there are others that you can find for yourself) are the interwoven stories of the cursing of the fig-tree (11:12-14, 20-23) and the cleansing of the Temple (11: 15-19), or those of the plot to kill Jesus (14:1-2, 10-11) and the anointing at Bethany (14:3-9). Here Mark has wrapped the story of the 12 year-old daughter of Jairus (5:22-24a, 35-43) round our story, which is that of another female, who has had her affliction for 12 years. We are surely meant to hold them together, but that must wait for another time. For the moment, I should like simply to read the text of 5:24-34, and leave you to make what you will of Mark's "sandwiching" of the two stories.

The story starts, through some skilful cinema direction on Mark's part, with a wide-angle lens revealing the oppressive crowd that hems Jesus in; then he focuses sharply on the woman, who is oppressed by something far worse than a crowd:

> *And a great crowd was following him,*
> *and they pressed in upon him.*
>
> *And a woman who had had a flow of blood for twelve years*
>
> *and had suffered much from many doctors*
> *and had spent all she had*
> *and had not been helped by it, but rather she had got worse . . .*

We are made to look at the crowd first, and our sympathy goes out to Jesus; but then immediately Mark forces us to look at the woman, and to grasp the extent of her sufferings. Indeed, there is really only one verse in the whole of this story that is not told from the woman's point of view. Her situation is dreadfully clear. Not only is this flow of blood an embarrassing humiliation; she is also ritually impure. In that culture, that meant that she was placed firmly on the margins of society. Look, for example, at this text from the Dead Sea Scrolls, to get a glimpse of the kind of treatment she might have received:

"As for the woman who suffers a seven-day flux of blood, she should not touch a man suffering from a flux, nor any implement that he touches, nor anything upon which he rests. But if she does touch (these things), she should wash her clothes and bath and afterwards she may eat (the pure food). At all costs she is [no]t to mingle during her seven days, so that she does n[o]t defile the camp of the Ho[ly O]nes of Israel . . . And the person that is keeping a record of the period of impurity, whether a man or a woman, is not to to[uch the menstruant] or the mourner during the period of uncleanness, but only when she is cleansed [from her unclean]ness . . ." (4Q274, as translated by Eisenmann in *The Dead Sea Scrolls Uncovered*, 1992, p.209).

And Mark further elicits our sympathy for the woman when he establishes that she had tried everything: she "had suffered much from many doctors, and had spent all she had, and had not been helped by it, but rather she had got worse". We shudder to think what kind of treatment she might have had to endure at the hands of the butchers who passed for doctors in her time and place.

> *hearing about Jesus,*
> *coming in the crowd behind him,*
> *touched his garment.*

> *For she said: If I just touch his garments,*
> *I shall be saved.*

Now we are wholly on her side, and even privy to her thoughts, as the evangelist goes on "hearing about Jesus", so that we actually know what motivated her, and are with her as she sneaks up "behind him", full of admiration for her daring, and understanding why she was so furtive in what she was doing. So much do we see it from her angle, thanks to the way Mark has told the story, that we almost fail to notice what she has done to Jesus: she has actually transferred to him her ritual impurity, but we are cheering her on at this stage. For we may also have noticed that she came "behind him", which in Mark's gospel is what disciples do; so the evangelist is telling us, not that we need telling by now, that she is a proper disciple, when she touches his garment.

> *And immediately the fountain of her blood was dried up*
> *and she knew in her body*
> *that she was healed of her suffering.*

See how the story continues to be told from her point of view, and how direct ("in her body") is her awareness of what has happened. At the same time, though, Mark tells us that the story has not quite ended, for, whereas in the previous verse she was hoping to be "saved", here she is only "healed"; instinctively we know that there is more to come here.

Now for the first and only time in the story we hear Jesus' viewpoint, and if we have been listening attentively we are rather curious to know (though we may feel that we can already guess) what his reaction will be to being made ritually impure. This is how Mark tells the story:

> *And immediately Jesus knowing in himself*
> *the power going out of him,*
> *turning round in the crowd said:*
> *who touched my garments?*

It is a curious way of telling the story. First of all we discover that Jesus "knew in himself", by which Mark presumably intends something different from the woman's knowing, which was "in her body", as we saw. Secondly, what he knows is the correlative of the woman's experience; she knew that her "affliction" had ended, while he knows that "power has gone out". Thirdly, see what he does *not* ask: it is not "who has gone and made me ritually impure?", but (unrealistically enough, as Mark emphasises: "turning round in the crowd"): "who touched my clothes?" This is the third mention of the crowd, and it serves to underline the oddity of the setting and of the question.

At this point we imagine a terrible silence, for Mark lets us picture Jesus turning towards the woman, and we see the event once again from her point of view; but the evangelist makes us wait, and, as so often in the gospel, the disciples are made to play the role of the slightly dim-witted "straight man", the one who has no real idea of what is going on here:

> *And his disciples said:*
> *do you see the crowd pressing upon you, and you say:*
> *who touched me?*

We hear their scarcely-veiled incredulity at the absurdity of the question, and are aware that only Jesus and the woman really have a grasp of the situation here; the disciples' jeering rejection of the question throws the two main characters into relief. But Jesus does not even listen to their question:

> *And he looked round to see the woman who had done this.*

Jesus has to know who has done it; but the Greek tells us something that is not often conveyed in the English versions, that Jesus *knew it was a woman who had touched him.* So now we very much want to know what she has to say for herself. And Mark duly obliges:

> *And the woman in fear and trembling*
> *knowing what had happened to her*
> *came and fell before him and told him all the truth.*

At this point, we know, if we had not already guessed, that all shall be well, for the woman comes forward "in fear and trembling", like those other women at 16:8; and this is certainly the appropriate response to the presence of God in the world. She then comes up and performs a gesture of worship, and spills the beans about the embarrassing truth. And we are now looking through her eyes once again, and perhaps waiting for the thunder: "Now look what you have gone and done, you stupid woman" might be how we should script the speech; except that fortunately Jesus does not have that kind of a scriptwriter. So there is going to be no thunder, as we knew from the fact that she "told him all the truth". And so it proves:

> *And he said to her:*
> *daughter, your faith has saved you.*
> *Go in peace, and be clean of your suffering.*

Jesus' reply starts with the beautiful expression: "daughter", at which we breathe a sigh of relief. It goes on indicating that something more than "healing" has happened to her; she has actually received what she was originally looking for, to be "saved": "your faith has saved you". And the story ends with the woman disappearing off-stage, never to be seen again, and leaving us full of rejoicing.

So it is a perfectly splendid story, and, as I say, tells us a good deal about both the evangelist and about Jesus (for the story can hardly have been invented), and their gentle empathy with women's problems. And there are many other stories which reveal this same attitude on Jesus' part, and most especially the gospels of Mark and John show a profound respect for women, which can no doubt be traced back to Jesus.

But it must be admitted, with hung head, that the Church has not always operated in this way. See, for example, the closing words of the gospel of Thomas:

> *But Simon Peter said to them: "Mariham should go out from among us,*
> *because women are not worthy of life". Jesus said: I shall draw her, to*
> *make her male so that she too may become spirit, and a living man, just*
> *like you males. Because every woman who will make herself a male shall*
> *enter into the Kingdom of Heaven". (Gospel of Thomas, 114)*

So what has happened in the later church that our treatment of women has been so different from that which we find in Jesus and in the gospels? Some would argue that the malign genius of Paul is the problem, and that he imposed his own particular hang-ups on the church as it moved from Palestine to the rest of the world, from Aramaic to Greek, and that he made us all into Male Chauvinist Pigs. Well, of course, it is never quite as simple as that, but since we are looking at the gospel and trying to see it as a liberating document, it may be worth examining any apparent example of unliberation in it.

iii) The Contribution of St Paul

It is very comforting to have someone to blame for the ills of our society, and in recent years the tendency has been to blame St Paul for the Church's attitude to women, with St Augustine as the second favourite. That distinguished African theologian is outside the compass of this book, but it will be worth having a look at St Paul's contribution to the position of women in the Church. At the same time we must remember that Paul and Augustine are both men of their time, and that as well as influencing church thought about women they also were products of what their peers thought and said. And if we in the Church have allowed women to be given an inferior position that is not what God wanted, then we must point the finger at ourselves, and not use others, and particularly not the safely dead, as scapegoats.

I am going to argue (you may not be surprised to learn!) that Paul is not quite as malign a figure as he is painted, and that he stood in the line of Jesus' unorthodox approach to women. The main texts that we shall deal with are those in 1 Corinthians, chapters 7, 11, and 14. There are other (and more embarrassing) Pauline texts, but I shall be arguing that they are not written by St Paul. You may regard that as a bit of sleight of hand on my part; but on the other hand, we have to admit that they are there in the New Testament, whoever is the author. So merely saying that Paul did not write them does not solve the problem.

For Paul, though, I am convinced (and I am not going to argue for it, but I think that you cannot understand his authentic letters in any other way) that his radical insight is that because of what God has done in Jesus, nothing else really matters. Therefore it was no longer important, for example, to aim at meticulous keeping of the Law; it was no longer important whether or not one had been born a Jew; it was no longer important what social class one belonged to. Therefore as far as Paul's attitude to women is concerned, the text I start with is Galatians 3:26-28:

> *For you are all children of God through faith in Christ Jesus.*

> *For as many of you as were baptised into Christ,*
> *have put on Christ*
> *In him there is no such thing as Jew or Greek,*
> *no such thing as slave or free,*
> *no such thing as male and female;*
> *for you are all one in Christ Jesus.*

In this letter, Paul is arguing against the trap into which at least some of the Galatian Christians have fallen, of scurrying back to strict observances of Jewish practices and feasts, and trying to persuade them that this is missing the point about what God had done in Jesus. The name of what God had done was "freedom", whereas the Galatians were trying to put on what he saw as a kind of slavery again. Jewish readers may find offensive the notion that cherished Jewish practices can be construed as "slavery"; they may be comforted, if not entirely cajoled, by the idea that it was more a question of what should be imposed on Gentile converts to Christianity.

As part of the argument, Paul reminds the readers of the significance of Christian baptism, that it makes those who are baptised into "children of God", not through any particular practices, but "through faith". And he uses the fact that after going down into the waters of baptism the new Christians put on a new garment, and he makes a metaphor out of that, and uses the word used for a Greek actor "putting on" the heavy costume that made the actor no longer the actor; he actually became the hero he (Greek actors were not generally women) was playing. So, Paul argues, the baptised person "puts on Christ", and it no longer matters who you are or what you have done or into what social class you were born: "you are all one in Christ Jesus".

This doctrine is an extraordinarily revolutionary one, and one that proved extraordinarily attractive; it is certainly part of the reason for the rapid spread of Christianity. And Paul here spells out the implications of this; he takes the three principal divisions of society in his day, and declares them annulled. The three divisions are those on grounds of ethnicity (Jew or Greek; in our day and in this country, he would certainly have said "black or white"), social class (slave or free; this was particularly daring, for the economy of the empire depended on the existence of cheap labour units in large quantities, but Christianity declared the equality of all humans), and gender (male *and* female; the conjunction "and", rather than "or", is presumably a reference to Genesis 1:27; but it would be revolutionary in both Roman and Jewish society to regard men and women as equals).

Now, as I say, I think that this doctrine of "radical equality" in Paul is his "bottom line", as they say nowadays. Another related doctrine that he frequently speaks of is that of the "new creation", which is a vision of a radically transformed world, looking like the way God sees it ought to be. Paul is trying to dissuade the Galatians from going back into what he saw as their ancient captivity, and to remain in the "new creation". As we listen to Paul, we need to remind ourselves that the ancient captivity is always more attractive than the uncertainties of the "new creation": we are more comfortable with the familiar, so the Letter to the Galatians is written also to us. The insight contained in these lines from Galatians are, so it seems to me, essential if Paul's gospel is to remain coherent: surrender the radical equality of all humanity, and you cannot any longer do justice to what God has done in Christ. Galatians is by a long way the angriest of Paul's letters; he is so angry that he omits the normal thanksgiving to God which comes in the early part of all his other letters. And the anger springs from their willingness to trade liberation for slavery.

So what about all the other Pauline texts, which the opponents of the ordination of women have triumphantly dredged up in our century? As I say, the principal ones are from 1 Corinthians; and that is important, because Corinth, as we shall see in the next chapter, was a special place, with its own special problems, and, although it is important not to exaggerate this, a part of the problem was what we should nowadays describe as an extremely permissive society; and Paul was not prepared to countenance sexual licence for those born again in Christ. So Paul when writing to Corinth has a particular situation in mind. Not only that, but Paul would have had no notion whatever that we might be reading his letters and trying to wring from them guidelines for our own conduct 2,000 years later. For Paul, like all the earliest Christians, was of the view that Jesus was to return any day now, and therefore he would have been politely incredulous had you told him that his hastily-dictated letters would have been of capital importance to the followers of Jesus in 1994. He might have written a good deal more carefully had he realised that this would be the case. Or he might not, for that was not his temperament; but the point for our purposes is that you must not play the game of Bible Bingo with the Scriptures, simply flinging quotations about with a view to trumping your opponents' aces. We have to read what he says to the Corinthians remembering that it is precisely to the Corinthians that he is writing.

So in chapter 7 Paul considers the question of marriage, and appears to offer, in response to various questions that the Corinthians have posed to him, a thoroughly debased theology of the union of man and woman, of which we have learnt in our day to have a much higher view. It seems as though Paul feels that marriage is no better than a way of avoiding fornication: "It is good for a man not to touch a woman; but because of fornications, let each man have his own wife, and each woman have her own husband". It must be said that we do not fully understand what Paul is talking about in this chapter; but as we read it, we must remember all the time what we have already said: first, that he was writing to a particular place with particular problems, and that the problems must have affected the answers he gives in way that we can no longer confidently reconstruct. And, secondly, as far as Paul was concerned, the Parousia could be here next Wednesday or next year, in which case there really is not much point in talking about marriage in the way we normally understand it.

Space does not permit a full examination of chapter 7, so I am going to ask you to read it for yourself, remembering those two points. And I will ask you also to see how carefully Paul insists on the equality of men and women, in verses 3, 4,12-16. And remember, too, that we cannot confidently translate all of the chapter. Scholars are divided on the meaning of verse 21, whether slaves are supposed to take advantage of the opportunity to gain their freedom or to remain as they are. Nor do we really know what is implied about the doctrine of marriage in verse 36. And however uncomfortable we may feel with verses 32-34, at least they remind us of a very important feature of St Paul, that he was head over heels in love with Christ; that relationship was the touchstone for him, and unless we keep that in mind all the time, we shall not be able to understand what he writes.

Let us go on to chapter 11, and a very difficult few verses, which it is worth printing in full; after each verse, I shall add a few words of explanation, aimed at elucidating Paul's view on women, which is what this chapter is supposed to be about.

> *I congratulate you that in every respect you remember me and as I handed down to you, so you remember the handings-down.*

Here Paul is clearly responding to a slightly complacent note in the Corinthians' letter to him, where they indicate how faithful they are to his teaching.

> *Now I want you to know that of every man the head is Christ,*
> *while the head of the wife is the husband,*
> *and the head of Christ is God.*

This is where those who proclaim the equality of the sexes start reaching for the delete button on their word-processor; but it may be worth noting here simply that "head" here does not mean "authority" in the Greek that Paul used, which is the way male supremacists have sometimes read this text, but "source". So Paul is here doing no more than reading off what, as far as he was concerned, the Bible said on the matter. He is *not* saying that men are entitled to control their wives, just as God is entitled to control Christ (a moment's reflection will convince us of the absurdity of Paul talking about God controlling Christ).

> *Any man who prays or prophesies with a thing on his head*
> *shames his head . . .*

This argument, which continues in the next two verses, is a hard one for us to handle; it may even have been a hard one for Paul to handle, as we shall see. Certainly, whatever precisely it means, it has to do with what is conventional in a particular society.

... while a woman praying or prophesying with head uncovered
shames her head. For it is just as if she were shaved.

Here the argument continues as in the previous verse; but we should notice that in these lines Paul assumes that, although men and women should dress differently, they may perform the identical liturgical functions. In other words it has to do with their clothing, not their role, in church. Incidentally, one of my childhood memories is of stopping on long car journeys to visit the Catholic church (which were never locked in those days, it would seem) in any town we passed through, to say a prayer, and the women of the family scrabbling for a handkerchief to cover their heads if they had no mantilla, scarf, or hat, with them. We no longer apply this teaching of St Paul's to women's dress, because, presumably, we have recognised that it is culture-bound, so the era of the dirty male handkerchief covering the female head is behind us. That is an important point for the way we read the New Testament and apply it to our situation.

So if a woman is not covered, let her be sheared.
But if it is a disgrace for a woman to be sheared or shaved,
let her be covered

Once again, this argument is from what Paul takes to be universally accepted convention; it does not, however, concern what a woman may *do* in the liturgy, but only how she is to be *attired*. A number of scholars argue that what Paul is attacking here is those who read into his "gospel of freedom" the licentious doctrine that "just about anything goes", which he certainly did not wish to maintain. In particular, it is possible that what worried him in the Corinthian situation was the practice of transvestitism or "cross-dressing", blurring the distinction between the sexes, and perhaps connecting with various homosexual practices. Corinth, the argument runs, was that sort of place. So we have to be careful how we read these lines if we are looking to apply them in our time and place.

For a man ought not to have his head covered,
being the likeness and glory of God.
But the wife is the glory of her husband;

for the man did not come from the woman
but the woman from the man.

And the man was not created for the sake of the woman,
but the woman for the man.

In these verses, the argument appears to rest on Scripture. Once again, it does not seem to speak of a proper chain of authority, so much as the origin of the human race; and here Paul's interpretation rests on his reading of the second account of creation, in Genesis 2:18-23. Once more, there is no question of women not being allowed to perform in the liturgy, but of how they are to be attired when they do so. Once again, we need to remember the Corinthian context. There were mystery cults at which, at least according to rumour, most undesirable practices took place, and it may well be that one of Paul's concerns here is to make sure that Christianity did not lay itself open to whispers of that sort.

> *Therefore the woman ought to have* exousia *on her head*
> *on account of the angels.*

As the argument runs, this verse sounds like a sort of triumphant conclusion, admitting of no further discussion. To us in the 20th Century it is not quite as simple as that. To be perfectly honest, we do not really know what it means. The word that I have transcribed as *exousia* should mean something like "authority"; it is the word used, for example, in Mark 1:27, to describe Jesus' authority over demons. Most translations render it as "veil". There is no evidence that the word can be used in this way; but it does seem (as we grope dimly after Paul's meaning) that it ought to refer to something that you put on your head. This may be because of the mystery religions that I mentioned earlier. Women who prophesied in their cults seem to have had their hair uncovered or dishevelled, and the "authority" may refer to something that prevents such indelicate behaviour.

The second puzzle here is what Paul means by "on account of the angels". There are various possibilities here: it may be that Paul is thinking of the "sons of God" in Genesis 6:2 who took wives from the human race, having noted their comeliness. Or it is possible that Paul has rather a negative view of angels, such as he reveals in Galatians.3:19. Or, finally, it might be that the Dead Sea Scrolls provide us with a clue, for in the "War Scroll" there is a list of various kinds of impure people who may not be with the armies when they march out to battle, "for the holy angels shall be with their hosts" (1QM VII; cf 1QSa II). At all events,Paul clearly thought there was some weight in the argument, even though we can no longer determine precisely what it was.

> *BUT there is neither woman without man*
> *nor man without woman in the Lord;*
>
> *For as the woman is from the man,*
> *so also the man is through the woman.*
> *But all is from God*

Our interest here, though, is in whether or not Paul has surrendered his belief in the equality of men and women that he emphasised in Galatians;

and quite clearly in these lines he is reasserting that equality. Whatever it is he wants women to wear, which, as we have indicated, may have to do with a fear of homosexual cross-dressing, he does not wish to go back on his assertion of the equality of the sexes. That is perhaps the most germane point in this extract: although Paul is clearly very agitated by whatever is going on in Corinth, he is not retracting his gospel of radical freedom.

> *Judge among yourselves:*
> *is it fitting for a woman to pray uncovered to God?*
>
> *Does not nature itself teach you that if a man has long hair*
> *it is a disgrace to him,*
>
> *whereas if a woman has long hair, it his her glory?*
> *For the long hair is given as a covering [protection?]*

The argument here is now no longer from Scripture, but from what looks like "natural law". Once again, although we do not find it easy to grasp how the argument runs, it is has nothing to do with the superiority of one sex over another, but with their *differences*. Now many feminist critics would argue today that stressing the difference between the sexes, or even their complementarity, is in fact a covert assertion of the superiority of men over women; all I am maintaining here, however, is that this is not necessarily a part of what Paul is saying. And certainly he is once again clear that women, just like men, may be expected to pray in public in the Corinthian church.

> *And if anyone wants to pick a fight,*
> *we do not have any such custom,*
> *and neither do the churches of God.*

If we have been scratching our heads so far, not certain how strong Paul's arguments are, it seems possible, on the evidence of this verse, that Paul is not too certain, either, for this is an argument from authority, foreclosing all further discussion; and you only do that if you are not sure that you have a very strong case.

What can we make of all this? Firstly, it was clearly a matter that Paul considered of great importance, for he wheels up a number of arguments to carry his point, and we do not find them all that overwhelming, and suspect that Paul may not have done either. Secondly, we find that we are not clear precisely what his point was, except that it had something to do with the proper clothes to be worn by men and by women. Why he was so emphatic about it, he does not say; but an informed guess (it is no more than that) links it to a fear of homosexual practices in the Corinthian church. Thirdly, we have seen that it is certainly not intended as anargument against the full participation of women in the liturgy. Nor has Paul retreated from the radical position he adopted in Galatians. Finally, we should see this as a particular case of a general thesis that runs throughout this book, that you cannot simply "read off" applications of Scripture, especially when it is a matter of reading a part of a letter, to our time and place, without first thinking of the context in which it was written, and the context in which we now propose to read it.

Now we can turn to chapter 14. Here, in verses 33-36, is an interesting passage, which seems like an irrefutable piece of evidence against Paul on the charge of Male Chauvinist Piggery:

> *As in all the churches of the saints*
> *let the wives be silent in the churches,*
> *for it is not permitted for them to babble;*
> *but let them be subordinated, just as the law says.*
>
> *And if they want to find something out,*
> *let them ask their own husbands at home,*
> *for it is disgraceful for a woman to babble in church.*
> *Or was it from you that the word of God came forth?*
> *Was it to you alone (masc.) that it has come?*

What on earth are we to say about this? Well, leave aside the question of its giving offence to feminist sensitivities; it really does not fit what Paul himself says in Galatians, nor does it square with what we have just seen in chapter 11 of the same letter, where women were quite clearly expected to "pray and prophesy" in the Corinthian church. It does not really fit the run of chapter 14, and interrupts the flow of verses 33a to 37. And it is not really in accord with the whole run of chapters 10 to 14, which concern themselves with correct behaviour in the liturgy, and, since chapter 12, with how the charisms are to be expressed in an orderly manner. In addition, the manuscript tradition is in some disagreement about where these verses belong.

You see already the way I am arguing: one strong possibility is that these verses were not written by Paul, but inserted later. It cannot have been too much later, or the verses would be missing from the manuscripts, rather than being found in different places in them. Why would anyone do such a thing?

To answer this question it is necessary to remember two things: firstly, that an interpolator would not see himself (it would be hard to imagine a *woman* inserting these lines!) as doing anything unfaithful to the spirit of Paul; he would be simply "saying what Paul would say to us today". The reason for that would simply be that the situation has changed, and therefore the teaching needed to change. What has changed? Quite simply, and this is the second thing we have to remember, Paul expected Jesus' Second Coming to be very soon indeed. If the time was short, as he firmly believed, then you only need a small number of limited moral perspectives. But by the end of the first century that belief was fading, indeed it was clearly mistaken, and in addition the Christians were a growing body who had to live in Graeco-Roman society as it was, including the social constraints on women. So I am going to argue, or rather, since space does not allow me to develop the case, simply assert, that our passage in 1 Corinthians 14, and all the other passages where "Paul" seems to have a negative view of women, are not in fact written by Paul. I shall give you the relevant passages, so that you can look through them for yourself, and make up your own mind. Firstly, there are two passages in what are called the Deutero-Paulines, that is to say Colossians and Ephesians. These letters are not universally accepted as being by Paul; probably they are by a disciple of the Apostle. The two relevant passages are Colossians 3:18 and Ephesians 5:21-33.

Then there are some passages in the "Pastoral Letters", the letters to Timothy and Titus, namely 1 Timothy 2:9-15; 3:11; 5:3-16; 2 Timothy 3:6-7; Titus 2:3-6. Now if you look at those, you will find that there are sentiments there which will make a feminist's blood boil. But no scholar today will argue that Paul wrote these letters. They come precisely from the time towards the end of the first century when the church was more settled, becoming more organised within itself, and more in need of accomodating with Graeco-Roman society.

Now at this point you may be feeling irritably that I am prepared to go to any lengths to acquit Paul on the charge of giving women an inferior position, and that any inconvenient texts I airily dismiss as "not by Paul". That is not quite what I have done: I have argued that Paul's basic position is that all people, of whatever race, social class, or gender, are radically equal under God. This radical equality is sharpened in Paul's case, and blurred in the case of the growing church of a generation or two later, by the expectation, not yet fulfilled, of an imminent Parousia or Second Coming. Others who stood, or regarded themselves as standing, in the tradition of St Paul, added "what the Apostle would have written in our situation".

But it is not quite as simple as that, and both feminists and those who oppose them may still wish to argue that, whoever wrote the material, it is still there in the New Testament, and presumably we are supposed to take it seriously. That is true enough; and to that argument I would make two responses. Firstly, it is yet another reminder of how we have to read the New Testament in context, reminding ourselves all the time that it comes out of a particular context, which affects the way it is written, and it comes into a particular context, which affects the way it is read; and you are simply not taking the Bible seriously if you do not bear both these contexts in mind. My second response is that even if you take the strictest texts in the Pauline corpus, those that most seem to downgrade women, and compare them with the situation of women (and children; for these texts appear in "household codes", where the church tries to lay down rules for proper order in families) in Graeco-Roman law, you will find that the Christian texts in fact work to protect the autonomy of women and children in a way that ran strongly counter to the prevailing culture. So we do take the texts seriously, but we also read them in context.

There is still a little more that we can say about St Paul and his attitude to women, before we leave the topic. Here we have to pick up hints that he drops when he mentions the names of particular women. In Philippians 4:2-3 he attempts to persuade Evodia and Syntyche to agree with each other, and describes them as "fellow-competitors of mine", using language that he uses of his own work as an apostle. So Paul seems to regard them as equals here. The same possibility is visible in Romans 16:1, where Phoebe is described as a "deacon" (*not* "deaconess" as the translations timidly have it) and as a *prostatis*. This is a very lofty title, and, once again, Paul seems by his language to suppose that Phoebe is his equal. Then there is a married couple, Priscilla (or Prisca) and Aquila, whom we meet at Romans 16:3-5, Acts 18:1-3, 18-21, 26, and 1 Corinthians 16:19. When they are mentioned, it is almost always the wife, Prisca, who is mentioned first. They worked with Paul, and ran house churches in Rome, in Ephesus, and in Corinth; nothing in what Paul says about them suggests that it must have been the husband, Aquila, who presided at such churches. Then there are some other women mentioned in Romans 16: Mary, Tryphaena, Tryphosa (these two may have been sisters, and their names could perhaps be translated as Gloomy and Grim-Face, charmingly enough!) and Persis. Once again, the language Paul uses of them suggests that he regarded them as doing the same sort of thing as he did.

A last name from Romans 16 is very interesting indeed. For in verse 7 Paul instructs the Romans to give greetings to two fellow-Jews of his (it seems), called Andronicus and Junia, whom he describes as "conspicuous among the apostles". Now for Paul, "apostle" was the highest title of all in the church. Andronicus is clearly a man's name, and Junias could be; it would be an abbreviated form of Junianus. The only difficulty is that this is not attested as a name. It could however be a *very* well attested woman's name, Junia, and if that is so, then Paul is according a woman very high status indeed.

Finally, it is often said that Paul was a misogynist old celibate, and that this accounts for the treatment of women in the church down the centuries. This may be so, but it need not be. The evidence for him being celibate is in two passages in 1 Corinthians (7:7-8; and 9:5,12). But the first of these refers not to celibacy, but to chastity, not to being unmarried, but to not having intercourse with his wife *at the moment*. And the second passage makes more sense if he *is* married, for it refers to his right as an apostle to take his wife with him, a right which he voluntarily forewent. So the evidence is not as strong as it may appear. Moreover Paul boasts in Philippians 3:4-6 that he was an observant Pharisee, and since celibacy was discouraged among the rabbis, who are the descendants of the Pharisees, it is more likely than not that he was married (though of course he could have been divorced or separated). And a possible identification has even been suggested. In Philippians 4:3 someone charged with bringing to an end the quarrel between Evodia and Syntyche is addressed as "Syzyge", which could be the vocative of a man's name, "Syzygos". However this is not attested as a name, whereas it is well known as meaning "yoke-fellow", or "spouse". So it is just possible that here Paul is addressing his wife; and it has been argued that if Paul had a wife still alive and still on his side, then Philippi would be a good place for his home-base. For it had excellent communications, it was centrally sited in the area of his missionary work, it was a church that he was evidently enormously fond of (to judge by the warm tone of his letter to them), and it might be that in Philippi we can locate his certainly long-suffering wife.

That is all highly speculative, of course, and it is time for us to draw this long chapter to a close, and with it venture five brief conclusions.

iv) Conclusions

i) The first thing that follows from what we said above is that both Jesus and Mark were clearly remarkably open in their attitudes towards women.

ii) Secondly, Paul was not necessarily male chauvinist. His basic stance, like that of Jesus, was that of the radical equality of men and women. He worked with women, spoke warmly of them, and may even have been married.

iii) There are signs that by the end of the first century the Church had retreated considerably from the fundamental insight of the equality of men and women. We have seen that among the reasons for this retreat may have been the fact that the Second Coming did not take place as expected, and the need to adapt to the expectations of the societies in which the late first century Christians found themselves.

iv) Words written by Paul, or attributed to him, and the Bible's patriarchal and androcentric attitudes, have certainly been used, in the history of the Church, for the oppression of women.

v) What does all this say to us about the ordination of women? Nothing very much, I fear, except that some of the arguments against the ordination of women have been shown, incidentally, not to have very much substance.

Finally, it seems to me that the Church is the poorer for our failure to make use of women's gifts. Perhaps if we could get right our language about God and about human beings, so that we are not driven always to see the male as the model, and if we could learn to enrich ourspeech about God with the female images that the Bible offers, then the solution to the problem about the ordination of women will become obvious. It may require also a rethinking of our theology of the priesthood, but that is another story; for the moment, let us simply notice that somewhere in the current agitation about the ordination of women the spirit of God is speaking. Our task therefore is in simplicity and prayerfulness and in all humility, to listen to Her.

Chapter 8

Building the Body of Christ

in a Multi-racial society

St Paul and the Corinthian community

Recently I was in Zimbabwe for a brief but illuminating visit, ten days spent working in a multi-racial parish in Bulawayo. As I listened to the people there wrestling with the problems they have been experiencing, ten years after independence, and as they shared with me the gains they have made, I was driven to reflect on the challenges and possibilities that face South Africa after our first democratic elections. But it is not merely Southern African countries that need to square up to the challenge of embracing the richness and the tensions that a society composed of many different cultures can offer. This morning's news on the BBC World Service told of killing, said to be inter-tribal in origin, in the capital of Ruanda, the relentless war being waged in what used to be Yugoslavia, and the British government being pressed to introduce legislation that makes racial harassment criminal. In a world made smaller by easy travel and sophisticated electronic technology, it has become more important than ever, perhaps more possible than ever, to learn respect for people of other races. It is liberating to discover that we are not diminished if we discover that they have something to teach us, and that in order to have peace you do not have to divide the world into different "tribes" or "cultures"; nor need we set aside homelands where different groups may live in sanitised isolation. For Christians, that is not the way God intended us to be, though we must hang our heads and shamefacedly confess that we have too often sinned against humanity in resisting the challenge of the pluralist world that God has created for us.

The problem of dealing with other races and other cultures is not a new one, and Christians have had to face it before. St Paul had to face it in Corinth, for example; there are several other examples of inter-tribal tensions in the Bible, but it seems worth looking at Paul's first letter to the Christians in Corinth to see if there are lessons to be drawn for our contemporary world.

The question we have before us, in almost every country in the world today is: how do you build the Body of Christ in a multi-racial community? The Corinth that Paul knew was a city where all sorts came together, and his Christian community bore the marks of their variegated origins. Not surprisingly, therefore, the Corinthian correspondence reveals signs of the tensions in that church. The answer Paul arrives at may be of enormous assistance to us today.

i) Corinth's geographical position

The Corinth that Paul knew was a Roman city, with an easily defended citadel; that is the reason why most settlements occurred in the ancient world, of course. In addition, it is greatly helped by its situation on the Isthmus of Corinth, the narrow strip of land that joins the two halves of Greece. So the North-South land route inevitably passed within its sphere of influence. And although it was not itself a port, it had two harbours, Lechaeum in the Corinthian Gulf, and Cenchreae on the East coast. The road to Lechaeum was fortified, for long-distance freight was as vulnerable to robbery and hijacking in thosedays as it is today. And goods that arrived at Cenchreae had inevitably to go through Corinth on their way to Rome, and pay taxes as they did so. Corinth, therefore was a conduit through which a great deal passed, with consequent "spin-off" for its inhabitants. I sometimes annoy some of my Gauteng-based pupils by claiming that it was the "Johannesburg of the ancient world".

Obviously one effect of this situation was that it was a very wealthy city. In addition to its commercial position, it had a regular tourist trap in that every other year the Isthmian games were staged nearby. These were second in importance only to the Olympic games, and, as today, that meant income for the host city. In addition to all this, Corinth exported bronze of a particularly valuable kind, which likewise swelled the coffers.

So Corinth was decidedly well-to-do; but in addition Corinthians were reputed in the ancient world to have a certain quality of being what you might call "street-wise" (it is here that the parallel with Johannesburg may be instructive), and there was a proverb to the effect that "not for every man is the journey to Corinth", implying that to survive there you had to know a thing or two. It was also, inevitably, a multi-racial city; they seem to have poured in from all parts of the world. There was a Jewish community there (the Jews have always been great travellers, or exiles, ever since the deportation to Babylon), whose tiny synagogue has been excavated, and representatives of many other religions as well.

Now in wealthy cities it is usually the case that the wealth is unequally divided; very often you find that the rich are scandalously rich, and the poor scandalously poor. Once again the example of Johannesburg comes to mind. Corinth seems to have been afflicted with this sort of divisiveness, complicated by class-distinctions as well. For the population of Corinth, so the social scientists estimate, was roughly one-third free, one-third slave, and one-third "freedmen", or slaves who had been given their emancipation or bought their freedom. The Roman empire depended on the cheap labour that the slave trade supplied, and large numbers of slaves seem to have passed through Corinth and to have been put to work there. So it was a community at least potentially at odds with itself. It was also, not surprisingly perhaps, something of a byword for sexual immorality. The story that Corinth had a temple of Aphrodite (the goddess of sexual love) where 1,000 sacred prostitutes lay ready to minister to the needs of devotees seems, alas, to be an invention of the geographer Strabo; but it shows at least the kind of city that it was thought to be.

The Church is not immune from its sociological setting, and the church in Corinth seems to have been a cross-section of the populace at large. Stephanas, mentioned at 1 Corinthians 1:17, and at 16:15-18, in a setting that suggests that he was important in the church, but not given respect by all members of the church, was a freedman, to judge by his name, and it is a sensible guess that Paul is dealing here with both class and race prejudice in the infant community. They must have been muttering "who does he think he is?" about Stephanas of the funny name and funnier background, and Paul has to tell them precisely who he is: one of those who have "made up for what you failed to do". There were also slaves in the Corinthian church (7:21); and there were, too, people with good Roman names like Crispus and Gaius, who in Romans 16:23 is described as Paul's host and the host of the whole Corinthian church, which means that he must have had a very sizeable house. And Paul also mentions Erastus, at Romans 16:23, describing him as the "city treasurer". Now archaeologists have excavated a pavement bearing the inscription "Erastus laid down this pavement at his own expense, in return for being aedile". An "aedile" was an official in the Roman administration who might well have been described as "city treasurer", and it is a pleasing thought that this might have been the very same Erastus. Even if it was not, our man must have been a fairly well-to-do member of the Christian group in Corinth.

As well as crossing social boundaries, the church certainly embraced several racial groups. There are Latin names and Greek names, and doubtless these conceal also people from several other nationalities who poured into Corinth from all over the Eastern Mediterranean. The Jews were in Corinth, as we have said (they were everywhere in the ancient world); and according to Acts it was Paul's pattern to preach first in the synagogue wherever he went, so it is reasonable to assume that some of his Corinthian Christians were Jews. Certainly Priscilla and Aquila were Jews (Acts 18:2).

So it was a rich mixture that Paul had to contend with in Corinth, and doubtless a heady one. This may account for the spectacular success of his preaching there, and it may indeed be the reason for the rapidity with which the gospel spread in those early days; all round the Mediterranean people were looking for hope and meaning and a sense of community that transcended boundaries; and the Christians offered it. We have already heard Paul proclaiming that in Christ "there is no such thing as Jew or Greek, no such thing as slave or free, no such thing as man and woman", and that challenge to all the established boundaries of the Roman-Greek universe will have exercised a powerful appeal.

Rich mixtures can however also be bad for the digestion, and the abiding impression of the Corinthian church that we gain from Paul's first letter to them is that there were fault-lines in it, and that there were cracks running along those fault-lines. It is nearly true to say that the only problem Paul is dealing with in Corinth is that of divisions in the church, as we shall see.

ii) Chapter 16

We can start our look at the letter (for reasons of space we shall only look at the first of the two Corinthian epistles here) with chapter 16. This is the final chapter, and because like Romans 16 it is intensely personal, and can sound like no more than a list of names, it is never read in church; but for our purposes it is very interesting. This is how it goes:

> With regard to the collection destined for the saints,
> as I commanded the churches of Galatia, so you must do:
>
> On the first day of the week, let each of you put something by, storing up whatever you earn, so that the collections do not wait until I come.
>
> When I come, those you choose, I shall send on their way with letters of recommendation to carry your gift to Jerusalem.
>
> And if it is right for me to go as well,
> they will go with me.

I shall come to you when I pass through Macedonia,
for I am going through Macedonia.

Perhaps I shall stay with you,
or even spend the winter with you,
so that you can send me on my way to wherever I am going next.

For I do not wish to see you now just in passing;
for I am hoping to remain some time with you, if the Lord allows.

I am remaining at Ephesus until Pentecost.
For a great and powerful door has opened for me,
and many are opposing me.

If Timothy comes, see to it that he is among you without fear,
for he is doing the work of the Lord just as I am.

Let no one treat him with contempt;
send him on his way in peace, so that he can come to me.
For I am waiting for him with the brethren.

As regards Brother Apollos,
I have often asked him to come to you with the brethren;
and no way was it the will [of Apollos? of God?]
to come at the present moment.
But he will come when the time is right.

Stay awake; stand firm in the faith, be manly, be strong.

Let all your things be done in love.

I beg you, brethren, you know the household of Stephanas,
how it is the first-fruits of Achaea,
and they have arranged themselves
for the diakonia of the saints,

that you too should be subordinated to people like this,
and to everyone who joins in the work and labours.

I rejoice at the presence of Stephanas and Fortunatus and Achaicus,
because these men have filled up your lack,
for they gave rest to my spirit and to yours.

So recognise people like this.

The churches of Asia greet you.
Aquilas and Prisca with the ekklesia in their house
greet you many times.

All the brethren greet you.
Greet each other with a holy kiss.

The greeting in my hand: PAUL.

If someone does not love the Lord, let him be anathema. Maranatha.

The grace of the Lord Jesus be with you.

My love with all of you in Christ Jesus.

This is extraordinarily interesting for us as we look for the "fault-lines" in the church. The instructions about the collection, a subject very dear to Paul's heart, is very odd: for the Corinthians are to lay something aside each Sunday. They are *not*, as you might expect, going to put it in the collection-plate, but store it up privately week by week. This strongly suggests a church in which they did not sufficiently trust each other to look after the money. This impression is strengthened somewhat by verse 3 where he speaks of "those you choose", using a word which might better be translated "those whom you judge to be of integrity", which implies that integrity was not a quality that you could take for granted in that church. And Paul himself clearly had to tread delicately, for he very carefully does not insist that he will accompany the collection to Jerusalem.

Then he shares his plans with them, and says he will come and perhaps spend the winter with them. That is interesting, because we learn from 2 Corinthians 1:15-2:4 that they complained that he had failed to fulfill this promise. We note that he says "many are opposed to me", and we may reflect that, on the one hand, anyone who preaches the gospel will find opposition at some point, and, on the other, Paul's temperament was such that he was forever finding people opposed to him.

Next he is in stern vein again, as he raises with them the question of Timothy and Apollos. Quite clearly he fears that Timothy may get a rough ride in Corinth in the visit that Paul mentioned in 4:17-21, and he wants them to be quite clear that Timothy speaks with the voice of Paul; and that he is coming straight to Paul after his visit, and will therefore be spilling any necessary beans directly.

Apollos is a different story; there was evidently an "Apollos faction" in Corinth, which had been in real or imagined rivalry with the "Paul faction" (for the evidence, see 1:12; 3:4,22; 4:1-6). Here Paul is acting to dispel any sense that he himself has prevented Apollos from coming to see the church where he had preached (Acts 18:24-26). He is careful to give him the honoured title of "brother", insists that, so far from preventing him, "I have often begged him to come to you", and that it was "not the will (whether of Apollos or of God it is not clear) to come now; he will come when the time is right".

Then the letter ends with, among other things, the reference to Stephanas, who may be a Corinthian Christian whom the other Corinthian Christians were inclined to make nothing of; and notice the repeated emphasis on love - I leave it to you to count up the number of times Paul mentions the word.

So chapter 16 presents us with a picture of a church in which there was little trust, a church for which Paul had great affection, but which needed to be reminded that they were not the only church in the world, and that there were other churches, in Asia for example, that he had to keep his eye on. We might ask ourselves, in conclusion, how Paul would have written to the Christians in our country today.

iii) The introduction to the letter

With these preliminaries, we can now do a rapid sweep through the letter as a whole, looking for the "fault-lines", and trying to relate what we read to the work of church-building that we are called to do where we live and worship.

Paul's letters follow the normal structure of letters in the ancient world. We are fortunate that an accident of the North Egyptian climate has preserved for us thousands of scraps written on papyrus, many of which are letters written in the cultural milieu to which Paul belonged; and the standard form of these letters is that they start with a greeting from the writer to the addressee(s). This is followed by a thanksgiving to the gods, then comes the main body of the letter, and the letter then normally ends with some personal salutations. We have already seen that chapter 16 of both Romans and 1 Corinthians have these final salutations, and you might like to look at the other letters of Paul to see the same phenomenon at work. The main body is the part that Paul has taken and made his own, a place where he can do creative theology, trying to work out on paper the implications of the gospel of Jesus Christ which he felt called to preach. But he always starts with the greetings and thanksgiving, generally at greater length than what we find in the papyri.

These introductions, and their accompanying thanksgivings, to Paul's letters are important in the way an overture is important in music: the themes are played to get our minds accustomed to them before we see how they are to be developed. So, for example, in Galatians where he is exceedingly cross, the introduction is brisk, and there is no thanksgiving, but verse 6 of the first chapter simply starts "I am astonished that so quickly you have altered from the one who called you in grace to another gospel".

The introduction to 1 Corinthians is not quite as cross as this, though at several points in the letter there are flashes of ill-temper from Paul. Nevertheless it is revealing. Paul insists that there are other churches in the world, by addressing himself to "the church of God that is in Corinth", an expression that he uses nowhere else, and emphasises the universality of the Church world-wide when he continues "along with all those who call on the name of Our Lord Jesus Christ in every place, theirs and ours".

Next we notice that Paul puts a good many of the words for what God has done into the *passive* voice. So for example, he addresses the Corinthians as "those who *have been* made holy", "those who *have been* called as saints"; he speaks of the "grace which *hasbeen* given to you", and says that he thanks God "because you *have been* enriched in everything by God . . . the mystery of Christ *has been* confirmed in you . . . so that you *are deprived* of no free gift, *receiving* [not exactly a passive, but implying the Corinthians' *passivity*] the revelation of Our Lord Jesus Christ". So the emphasis all the time is not on what the Corinthians have done, but on what has been done to them: "he will confirm you irreproachable to the end . . . God is faithful, through whom you *have been* called".

It may be worth setting out the opening verses of the letter together:

Paul, called an apostle of Christ Jesus
through the will of God
and Sosthenes the brother,
to the church of God which is in Corinth,
to those who have been sanctified in Christ Jesus,
who have been called to be holy,
with all those who call upon the name of our Lord Jesus Christ,
in every place, theirs and ours,
grace to you and peace,
from God our Father and the Lord Jesus Christ.

I give thanks to my God always about you
over the grace of God which has been given to you in Christ Jesus

because in everything you have been enriched in him,
in every logos and in every gnosis,

as the witness of Christ has been strengthened in you.

So that you are not lacking in any charisma
waiting for the revelation of our Lord Jesus Christ.

And he will indeed strengthen you until the end,
[making you] irreproachable
on the day of our Lord Jesus Christ.

God is faithful, through whom you have been called into the koinonia of his
son Jesus Christ our Lord.

I have left in the original Greek the key-words *"logos"* (word, but also meaning reason and rationality, and the rational principle on which the universe is constructed), and *"gnosis"* (knowledge, particularly of a specialist sort, on the possession of which the Corinthians seem to have prided themselves) and *"koinonia"* (partnership, union, or communion - in other words precisely what the Corinthians lacked in their admiration for their own *logos* and *gnosis*).

From the beginning, therefore, if we are attentive to what Paul has to say, we may be starting to wonder whether the problem at Corinth may not have been that they had too exalted a view of themselves, forgetting that what counted was not their spectacular achievements, but what God in Christ had done for them. Hence the emphasis on "grace" and God's free gift; and here we find the first mention of some words that are going to be of importance in the letter as a whole. Two of these words may have been readily on the lips of the Corinthian Christians. In Greek they are *logos* and *gnosis*, which mean, respectively, "word" and "knowledge", but are both wider than that, and have a background in both Greek and Jewish culture. Both of them refer to characteristics on which human beings may tend to pride themselves, and part of Paul's task in this letter will be to say that there is such a thing as both *logos* and *gnosis* without allowing the Corinthians to suppose that they can get to God all by themselves. This is an observation that is important not merely for 1st century Corinth, of course; it has impact also on our world at the end of the second millenium. And it is a fair bet that this introduction was not at all what the Corinthians were expecting; reading between the lines, it is possible to detect an eminently human complacency about where they stand, which Paul is doing his best to shatter constructively.

iv) Paul's sources of information

It is quite clear from 7:1 that Paul is writing in reply to a letter that the Corinthians had written to him. At various points (7:1; 7:25; 8:1; 12:1) Paul uses a phrase that means something like "now, about . . .", introducing his response to certain questions that they had raised. But we notice that the letter is well under way by the time he deigns to answer them. A good deal of what he wants to say is that they were really not worried about the things that ought to have worried them, rather as if people in South Africa might have worried about eating meat on Fridays but not about *apartheid*.

The fact is that Paul has heard from other sources, such as "Chloe's people" (1:10) about the problems on which their letter had been silent. And there have been other reports, which may have come from the same source or from some other, about incest (5:1), and about litigation (6:1), and about behaviour at the eucharist (11:18), and perhaps also about dissent on the matter of resurrection (15:12), which have come to Paul other than through the Corinthians' letter. So before he replies to them he offers a few shots across their bows about what is *really* wrong with them. We can only imagine how they will have felt when this letter was read out at their weekly gathering; but we must assume from the fact that they bothered to preserve it that they thought he was broadly right, even if they were a bit shaken by his attitude.

v) *The problem at Corinth*

What Paul saw, and what they seem completely to have failed to see, was that the heart of their problem was their divisions, and the fact that they had far too high an opinion of themselves. As we read the letter (and I hope that it will be open in front of you as you read this chapter), that is the one thing that stands out above all. For Paul a divided church was a contradiction in terms; and his objection to the Corinthian Christians was precisely that they had not noticed the problem (and as we read we must ask ourselves what the problems are in this country today that *we* have failed to notice). The difficulty may have been compounded by the fact that, assuming that a sizeable number of them were converts from outside the Jewish tradition, they had no Old Testament background that he could rely on, so sexual chastity, for example, was not a virtue that you could take for granted, nor an ideal that they would automatically aim for.

It was divisions, however, that Paul objected to. They had evidently formed themselves into factions in that church, and were marching up and down with placards reading "Viva Apollos", "Vote for Kephas", and "Paul's my main man" (1:12). It may be possible to reconstruct what these different parties stood for: Apollos was "powerful in biblical studies" (Acts 1:24), and came from Alexandria, where they had a particular way of reading the Old Testament. Kephas (the Aramaic for Peter, as you probably know) had, according to Galatians 2:11-14, got on the wrong side of Paul for an inconsistent attitude to Jewish customary law; and Paul, of course, was Paul. As we read the letter, and notice the number of times we see apparently key terms like "wise", "knowledge", "weak", and "logos", we can guess that at the root of the divisions there was a particular way of looking at reality. But the key thing is not what the different parties stood for, but that there were parties at all in the church.

It seems very likely that the party nicknamed "the strong" may have been a shade over-enthusiastic in their reception of Paul's gospel of freedom. We can see from Galatians that central to Paul's preaching was the notion that we are no longer under the constraints of the law. And Corinth being the sort of place it was, the Corinthians may have interpreted liberty as licence, and formed for themselves the view that in Christianity, "anything goes". So in chapter 6, Paul uses the slogan: "anything goes for me", he says in verse 12, and gives the answer: "yes - but not everything is helpful". Then he repeats the slogan, and comments "yes - but no one can say what 'goes' for me". Here he is talking about fornication, and trying to get them used to the idea that it is simply incompatible with membership of the body of Christ.

In chapter 10 Paul repeats their slogan while attempting a discussion of how to handle the difficult question of food offered to idols: "anything goes", he says at verse 23, and replies: "yes - but not everything is helpful". Then he plays with the slogan again: "anything goes", and comments "but not everything builds up". And that is the solution to the difficulty: Christians *are* free because of what God has done in Christ, but they do not have only themselves to consider, for Christianity is something you do in solidarity with others; you have to "build up". Paul uses here the metaphor of a building to describe the group of Christians; elsewhere, as we shall see, he speaks of the church as a "body", which turns out to be a very serviceable metaphor for his purposes. But the idea is the same, that Christians need to think of others, and so control their freedom.

This is precisely what they have failed to do in Corinth. The man who committed incest (5:1), and the rest of the Christians who reacted so casually to it (verse 2), those who committed fornication or took each other to court (chapter 6), the ones who carelessly implicated themselves in idol-worship (chapters 8 and 10), those who - worse still! - had a low opinion of Paul (9:1), those who practised class distinctions at the eucharist (11:18-21 - see below), and even questioned the Resurrection (chapter 15), all these revealed a complacency about where they were before God and a divisive selfishness about their own private peccadillos that could end by destroying the Christian community.

An excellent example of their divisions was precisely at the eucharist, which ought to function as the symbol of Christian unity. Paul is very cross with them in the following verses:

> *But in giving these instructions I do not praise you;*
> *for your gathering is not for the better, but for the worse.*
>
> *For in the first place, when you come together as an ekklesia,*
> *I hear that there are schismata among you,*
> *and to some extent I believe it.*
>
> *For it is inevitable that there should be sects among you,*
> *so that the reliable ones among you may become evident.*

For when you come together into the same place,
it is not to eat the Lord's Supper,
for each brings his own supper, and gets on with eating it,
and one goes hungry, while another is drunk.

Do you not have houses for eating and drinking?
Or do you despise the ekklesia of God?
and do you humiliate the have-nots?
What am I to say to you? Am I to praise you?
In this I do not praise you.

You will notice that in this terrible tirade I have left two words in the original Greek: "ekklesia", and "schismata". Paul is making a really serious point here: and "ekklesia" is the word that we often translate as "church", but it refers to the group "called out", and translates the Hebrew *qahal*, which referred to God's people in the desert, among other things. Against that Paul uses the word "schismata", connected with the English word "scissors", and the direct ancestor of our word "schism". Significantly enough, 1 Corinthians accounts for exactly half the uses of the word "schismata" in the New Testament. It means divisions, and for Paul you *cannot* have an *ekklesia* with *schismata*. And here are the Corinthians parading their divisions at the eucharist, which should be the symbol of unity! It may be that there is a class thing here; for those who arrive early may very well be those who do not have jobs to come from, the wealthier Christians, possibly those who were more congenial to the owner of the large houses where the Christians met (for they had no church as such, and were a large group, probably several hundred strong). Whereas, it may well be, the poorer Christians came late, and found the meal already eaten, and some of their "fellow-Christians" already drunk. This would be a horrible parody of Christian unity.

Once again, we need to read Paul's indictments, and ask where the cap fits in this country today; for wherever the Church has been church, the problems, or rather the problem, to which Paul points, has surfaced. Now we need to look in greater depth at the answer Paul gives.

vi) Paul's answer to the problem

Paul's answer to the problem comes in several bits. Firstly, he tells his Corinthians a parable, which he relates with a touch of comedy. It was a parable which others had also used in the ancient world, but Paul employs it with considerable originality:

For the body is not one limb but many.
Suppose the foot says "Because I'm not a hand,

I don't belong to the body,"
does that make it not a part of the body?

And suppose the ear says: "Because I am not an eye,
I don't belong to the body",
does that make it not a part of the body?

If the whole body was eye, where would the hearing be?

If the whole thing was hearing, what about the sense of smell?

But in fact God has placed the parts of the body each of them in the
position in the body where God wanted them.

And if they were all just one limb, where would the body be?

The idea here is that all parts belong together; and Paul would have his Corinthians nudging each other with appreciative grins at the idea that a foot or an eye could pretend not to be a part of the body. Until, that is, they realised that he was talking about them. This is a parable directed at those who cannot cope with the richness of humanity, the glorious diversity of the body of Christ, against those who would argue for *apartheid* of any kind in the Church or outside it.

Secondly, Paul tries to shame them out of their complacency. Imagine how they will have felt as this was read out in their gathering:

For look at your call, brethren;
not many were wise, as humans understand the term,
not many were powerful,
not many were nobly born.

But it was the foolish things [morons] that God chose
in order to shame the wise.
And the weak things of the world that God chose
in order to shame the strong.

And the unborn of the world and the despised that God chose,
the nonentities, so that he might bring the "entities" to ineffectiveness,
so that there might be no human boasting before God.

As a result you are in Christ Jesus,
who became Wisdom for us from God
and justification and consecration and redemption,

so that, as it is written,
"let the one who boasts boast in the Lord".

Another example might be the schoolmasterly reproach of 15:34, or the various places where he simply treats them as refractory children: look for instance at the rebuke in 3:1-2, and compare 2:6. Or read 4:6 and 21 from the point of view of people who rather fancied themselves as the latest thing in sophistication (and see the reference to their "childishness" concealed in 13:11 and 14:20).

Thirdly, Paul emphasises the cross, setting its "foolishness" against their smart but sterile philosophical sophistication. Read slowly through the whole of 1:18-2:5, and see how the cross functions in his argument.

Fourthly, Paul preaches to them about love. Chapter 13, that loveliest of hymns which flowed from Paul's pen, fits the Corinthian situation perfectly, though it may not have been originally written to go here, for chapter 12 would run nicely into chapter 14. Nevertheless, it fits the flow of his argument well enough. It is all very well priding themselves on their charisms; but if charisms are like so many "badges", which they can point to in order to demonstrate that they have "made it" as Christians, then they do more harm than good. Chapter 13 is the answer to all the Corinthian problems, which is really only one problem, that they are divided. They prided themselves on their "knowledge", and Paul insists that what they need is love, not degrees. And the difference, he tells them sharply at 8:1, is that while knowledge "puffs up" (this is a word he uses several times, apparently to indicate the insubstantial self-importance of his opponents), love "builds up". Love, that is to say, is for real. And at 8:13 he offers them a practical demonstration of what it means: "so if food makes my fellow-Christian to stumble, then I shall never ever eat meat again, so as not to make my fellow-Christian stumble". It is not sophistication that counts, but love. And Paul was a genuinely affectionate person. Though he gets furious with his Corinthians, you cannot miss his fondness for them, as in 4:14: "I do not write this to make you ashamed, but just giving a warning to my children whom I love very much".

Lastly, what is almost the same thing, Paul turns their minds to Christ. So at 2:2 he reminds them of the original gospel that he preached to them: "Jesus Christ, and him crucified" (and compare 11:23ff and 15:1ff, recalling to their minds the heady days when they first heard the gospel). At 1:12, when rebuking them for the slogans: "I belong to the Apollos-party", "I belong to the Kephas-party", "I belong to the Paul-party", Paul adds, not a fourth party, but a grim little joke of his own, reminding them of the party they should *all* belong to: "I belong to the Christ-party". And he talks of his work and Apollos' as that of builders, who must have a foundation: "no one can lay down any other foundation than the one that has been laid down, which is Jesus Christ" (3:11, and compare the soaring lyricism of 3:21-23). It is this conviction that Christ is central that grounds his appeal at 11:23-27 to what Jesus did on the night before he died.

The fact is that Paul is a man obsessed with Christ. Count the number of references to Jesus in the first ten verses of this letter. What God had done in Christ, and what Jesus had done to Paul, was really the heart of his theology, and therefore the main plank of his approach to the problems that his Corinthians were posing him.

The solution that Paul *never* considers is the non-answer that some churches (all churches, at different times?) embraced in South Africa, of saying "different races, and different cultures imply different churches". One can see that it would have been tempting; for there were considerable cultural differences in the group that made up the Corinthian followers of Jesus; and the probable size of the group meant that they could not easily all meet in one house; even the largest of the Roman villas excavated in Corinth could probably not have fitted all the Christians who were there in Paul's day. The option of separate churches, in a flight from diversity, is too common a human response; but it is not what God asks of us, nor is it in our own best interest. I remember that when a friend of mine, the parish priest of a largely Zulu parish, was killed in a car-crash recently, the funeral was a marvellous affair, death celebrated as African people know how to celebrate it, with great sadness and joy, and singing and dancing of just the right kind. They had an all-night vigil, beginning and ending with mass, and it was a moving and prayerful occasion. But the small white community, whom the priest had served devotedly, did not come, presumably fearful or foolishly uncertain of their welcome at the service. And they would have learnt so much if they had been there. The African people were far too polite to comment on their absence, of course; but they must have wondered how white people express grief and gratitude, or even whether they feel such things. It was an opportunity squandered.

Paul's answer is to embrace the richness of living in a diverse and multi-racial community. He does not express it quite like that, of course; instead, he speaks of the "body", which is united precisely in being diverse, a profound truth that the sin of *apartheid* (which in different ways we all commit when we "prefer to be with our own") simply ignores. The body is a very useful term for Paul in this letter, and we can conclude with a brief look at how Paul uses the idea.

vii) The "body" in 1 Corinthians

"Body", both in English and in Greek, can have a number of different meanings. It can refer to the body of an individual, or to the "body politic", the state, or we can speak of a "governing body". Then in Christian theology we speak of the "body of Christ", which can refer equally to the Church, the eucharist, or Jesus' risen body. And Paul uses the word "body" in all these senses as he tries to tackle the problem of disunity in Corinth. A body that is operating properly values all its parts equally, he says, in the parable in chapter 12, even giving particular honour to those bits that are less highly regarded (12:23). If we think of a physical body, then this argument is rather hard to follow; if, on the other hand, we recognise that Paul is really talking about the "body" that is the Christian Church, then it becomes quite clear: Paul is lecturing those Corinthians who had too exalted a notion of themselves on the importance of the humblest and least educated or least well-to-do members of the Church, precisely those poor and marginalised that the Church has concerned itself with most in the course of its history (at least when it has been functioning properly). It is this which explains Paul's anger in chapter 11, about the invidious class-distinctions at the eucharist. The eucharistic body of Christ is "one bread", and is mortally offended if there are divisions and cliques. This is message is not just for first century Corinth!

viii) Conclusion

Division, then, is the name of the problem at Corinth; and the answer to the problem is to embrace the richness of living together in Christ, rejoicing in individuality and difference. I think that this is a really important notion, for it seems to me that Paul's central theological insight, and the main doctrine of Romans, is not the slogan about "justification by faith"; that has been thrown too sharply into focus by Reformation controversies and their hangover. Paul's main contribution to our Christian theology is the insight that God in Christ restores the unity of all creation. Hence the importance in 1 Corinthians of the idea of "body". Paul brings this out skilfully, tracing the connection with Resurrection, in 1 Corinthians 15:20-28, which I commend to you for reflective and prayerful reading. Or you might consider the use of the word "all" in 1 Corinthians 9:19-23. What Paul seeks to restore in Corinth, because of this central insight of his, is the shattered *koinonia*, for Christianity is nothing if it is not partnership or communion. It calls, as chapter 13 of 1 Corinthians so memorably hymns, for love. And love is not anything starry-eyed or easy, but the hard discipline of labouring to build community. That is something that we need in South Africa today; and perhaps there is nowhere in the world where it is not required. 1 Corinthians is a letter for our times.

Chapter 9

Conclusion

Why read the Bible in
this country today?

As we come to the end of this book, it is my hope that you see more reasons than before for reading the Bible in this country today, wherever "this country" is for you, and whatever is your "today". But it may help to sum up what I have been trying to do if we look afresh at the question of reading the Bible.

i) Reasons for not reading the Bible

It may be sensible to start by considering reasons *against* reading the Bible in these days and in this place. This may have the advantage of bringing a certain clarity to the question. I shall offer four possible reasons, and you may profitably exercise yourself in thinking of others.

The first reason that people offer is that "it's all a pack of lies". This, I take it, is code for "I have heard that biblical scholars say that not every word in the Bible is literally true, but must be understood according to what kind of document it is". That is to say that over the last two centuries or so, scholars have been reading the Bible in a scientific way, exposing it to modern historical criticism, using the findings of scientific archaeology, palaeography, linguistics, and so on, not to mention the physical sciences, and learning to appreciate it in a way that is quite different from that of the ordinary reader. An example of some people's anxiety about the Bible might be the question of evolution. Scientific discoveries and theories about the origin of our world and of human life seem to some people to conflict with what is said, for example, in the pages of Genesis. And there are those on both sides who feel that it must be one or the other. *Either* the physical sciences are right *or* the Bible is right. Within Christianity there are what are known as "fundamentalists". This term is notoriously difficult to define, but would probably include the view that the Bible is literally true, and contains no mistakes. Such people might characteristically start off with the position that if science does not agree with the Bible, then so much the worse for science. Others will take the opposite view: that science has replaced the Bible, which is no longer required for the modern educated person; and if the pages of Genesis seem to contradict what scientific investigators have discovered or hypothesised, then into the dustbin the pages of Genesis must go.

Actually both sides are wrong, because neither of them understands what we are doing when we read the Bible. If you have managed to read all the way through this book, you will have no difficulty in grasping that the Bible is, at any rate as far as I am concerned, a document of immense importance; but its importance does not depend on its excellence as a scientific treatise. It is no such thing, nor does it set out to be. Therefore to call it a "pack of lies" is the kind of thing journalists or adolescents do when they are trying to cause a flutter.

Secondly, it is suggested that the Bible is, or fosters, a dangerous illusion. The dangerous illusion, I suppose, is that there is a God and that God can be trusted to run the universe in an acceptable way; and this would be an illusion if there were no God, or not a God interested in our affairs; and it would be dangerous if it led us to give up our responsibility for making the world a better place. The question of whether it is an illusion is not one that falls within the aims of this book, though it must be clear that I do not regard the "God-story" as an illusion. And certainly anyone who reads the Bible as a whole, and with an open mind, must concede that it has its collective feet firmly on the ground; its stories are flesh-and-blood stories about real human beings whom we can recognise and identify with, but in whose lives it is possible to discern the working of an over-arching purpose.

A third objection to the Bible is that it presents a God who commands immoral things. That is perhaps putting it too strongly, but if you read these verses in Psalm 137 (which are not often read in church, by the way!), you might blench a little:

> *O daughter Babylon, you devastator!*
> *Happy shall they be who pay you back what you have done to us!*
> *Happy shall they be who take your little ones*
> *and dash them against the rocks!*

We need to know that the Bible has material of that sort in it; and we may not feel entirely comfortable with it, but I take it that we can say at least two things about it, that it gives powerful expression to the feelings of the human heart (which is a good thing; the bad thing is when you act out the feelings), and that no one in their right mind would be inspired by these words to go on a bout of baby-bashing.

Or read that compelling story in Genesis 22, the "binding of Isaac". It might be possible to read this as revealing a God who demands bloody sacrifices, a God from whom all decent people would revolt. But the story, one of the most moving in the whole of world literature, is not about child-sacrifice but about the abiding faith of Israel that whatever it seems like, "God will provide". There are a good many disedifying tales in the Bible, but that is because all human life is there. If you want, as people have wanted at various stages and in various guises down the ages, a sanitised form of the Bible, made acceptable to refined sensibilities, then it is not the Bible that you want, nor is it really God that you are looking for. And, it must be added, you will end up with a thoroughly tedious, and rather short, collection of fragments.

Fourthly, there is an objection that runs: you should not read the Bible because religion does more harm than good. Religious people, so the argument would go, are responsible for a good deal of the ills of our world, and the world would be a more peaceful place without it. *Apartheid*, for example, was the brainchild of devout Christians, and so were the Inquisition and the Crusades. All perfectly true, but, once again, you only have to sit down and read the Bible without prejudice to see that all these aberrations are the products of the human heart, which (at its worst) can be vicious, grasping, homicidal, racist, and a thousand other things. And religious people have at different times used religion as a peg on which to hang their unpleasant tendencies, and sometimes as a sanitiser, to legitimate them. It does not, however, follow that religion is the cause of such evil. The Bible, take it all in all, offers a powerful challenge to those who embrace evil, and it asserts that evil shall not ultimately conquer.

ii) What is the Bible?

As I say, you can probably think of a good many more reasons why you should not read the Bible; but it may be worth advancing our investigation a little by looking at a related question, namely what precisely the Bible is. That may seem to you a foolish question, because so obvious, for the Bible is a book, indeed some would say *The* Book, and there it is, inspired by the Holy Ghost, between the covers of your Authorised Version, or RSV or NIV or whatever, and there an end on't.

But it is more complicated than that. As a matter of fact, we cannot be absolutely sure of the precise text of either the Old Testament or even the New Testament in some places. One of the things revealed by the discovery of the Dead Sea Scrolls in Qumran was that the people who stored their library in the caves there knew of several - at least three - different traditions of the text of what we call the Old Testament. The same scrolls reveal a good deal of freedom with the way they handled the text, changing and adapting it where necessary. Therefore we cannot with confidence say, for example, which of two texts the prophet Jeremiah actually wrote. And in that case the question poses itself, if you take too rigid a view of inspiration, which of the versions represents inspired truth?

Then again, unless you have gone to the trouble of learning Hebrew and Greek and Aramaic you are dependent on a translation for your knowledge of the Bible. And translations, obviously, differ from each other, sometimes by quite a lot. Would we want to claim that the translators are inspired? Presumably not, no matter how good we thought they were at translating.

So the question that seemed so simple turns out to be rather elusive, like nailing jelly to the ceiling. The Bible is vague in a number of maddening ways, which seem to resist the precise categorisation that fundamentalism demands. Let me therefore suggest a possible way of understanding what the Bible is.

First of all, the Bible is the Church's gift to itself. This, the Church decides, are the documents that speak to us of God. They are not written by God, but by human beings who had the limitations of their time and culture. And the Church, and for that matter the Jewish authorities, took their time in making up their mind which documents they wanted to regard as authoritative. For example, for Qumran, and for at least one writer in the New Testament, the Book of Enoch had that status, but Jews and Christians no longer include it in their Bibles. And many of the documents in the Bible were edited from pre-existing material, to present a particular point of view (which of course raises the further question about inspiration: who was inspired - the original authors or the later editors?). So it is safest to start not with the inspired writers, but with the Church (leaving aside for this purpose the process by which Jews came to regard certain documents as authoritative); and the Church spent several centuries looking at various documents, and eventually deciding that some of them did, while others did not, speak to them of what God was like and of what God had done in Jesus. The documents that compose the Bible are therefore in an important sense products of the Christian community, even those not written by Christians.

Secondly, the Bible is a *library*. It is a collection of many different types of document. There is history, like the books of Samuel and Kings; there are racy narratives such as some of those in the first 11 chapters of Genesis; there are obscure rules about diet and what priests should wear or how to build a tabernacle. There are songs of several different types. There is the erotic love-poetry of the Song of Songs, funny stories like the Book of Jonah;

and weary agnosticism such as you find in Ecclesiastes (aka Qoheleth), or the angry questioning of the Book of Job. Each of these types of literature, and the many others that the Bible contains, needs to be examined on its own merits. So even a simple question like "Is the Bible true?" can only be answered by first asking "what kind of truth is appropriate to literature of this kind?" Homer's Odyssey, that great epic of Greek literature, is *true*, for it relates the striving of the human heart to return home, and a good many other things besides; but it is not true in the sense that it would do for a newspaper report. Very little of the material in the Bible would count for a newspaper report; but that does not meant that it is false, only that we need to be sensitive to the kind of literature we are dealing with. Otherwise we shall be in danger of missing what God is really saying to us in its pages.

Thirdly, this library records, not history as such, but the struggle of the human race with God, and God's search for the human race. We humans do not grasp the reality of God just like that; at different times and places, the mystery of God can seem beyond our reach and occasionally simply absurd. We look at the facts of history, and wonder sometimes if there can possibly be a benevolent intelligence running the universe; and we want there to be. Well, that painful wondering and that desire for God, and indeed all the moods of the human race, are in the Bible, woven together in the shape of our journey towards the creator.

At the same time, the constant factor which unites the whole Bible is the fidelity of God. The entire library "documents" God's patient searching for humankind, the refusal to be deterred by human infidelity and rejection, the striving to fashion meaning out of human history, in partnership with the human race.

One way of grasping this is to note that in the Bible's first chapter (Genesis 1:2) the Spirit of God (at least that is one way of translating the Hebrew) is pictured hovering creatively over the chaos, while the last chapter offers another vision of the work of God (Revelation 21:1-5):

> *And I saw a new heaven and a new earth.*
> *For the first heaven and the first earth went away, and the sea is no more.*
> *And the holy city, new Jerusalem,*
> *I saw coming down out of heaven from God*
> *made ready like a bride adorned for her husband.*
> *And I heard a great voice from the throne, which said :*
> *"See the tent of God with humankind,*
> *and he will pitch his tent with them,*
> *and they shall be his peoples and he himself God with them will be.*
> *And he will wipe away every tear from their eyes,*
> *and death will not be any more,*
> *nor mourning nor weeping nor suffering shall be any more.*
> *The first things have gone away".*

This beautiful vision is an utterly appropriate way for the Bible to end; for that is what God is doing with the human race, constantly creating anew, getting rid of the "old" and bringing in the perpetually "new", so that the human race, that is all of us, and the whole of creation, may come to be as beautiful as we could be, "like a bride on her wedding-day". It is not a remote God, this God of the Bible, but a comrade-God, one who "pitches tent" with us, a God who is with the people of God, putting an end to all their suffering, and to the last great enemy, which is death. That is a vision to excite us, and a reason for reading the Bible.

iii) Reasons for reading the Bible

We have almost answered the question "why read the Bible?" Indeed, I hope that this whole book has been an answer to the question. But we can round it off by pointing specifically to some considerations that might drive us to reading the Bible.

First of all, the Bible is a privileged means of access to God. God is everywhere, the mark of the creator God is left all through creation, and in the slogan of St Ignatius Loyola, who founded the Jesuits, we look to "find God in all things". Nevertheless, in the Bible, which we have described as "the Church's gift to itself", we have a collection of documents that give us a unique way into the mystery of who God is and what God is about, and the different ways in which human beings respond and co-operate, or fail to co-operate.

Secondly, though, the Bible offers us no magical solutions to the problem of living; nothing cheap or easy is on offer here. The Bible is hard to read, it is a product of its time and place; it is uncomfortable, and makes us shift uneasily in places, and mutter "it would have been better not to have said that". And, since it is dealing with the mystery of God, and the human intellect can only approach God by negation, there are many contradictory theologies in the Bible, many inconsistencies. And we need to face the inconsistencies, and wrestle with the mystery. For human life is a mystery, harsh and uncomfortable in places, but always worth the struggle; and if we run from it the mystery will still be there.

Thirdly, the story, in a phrase that I have used several times in this book, is one that "invites us aboard". The Bible story (for there is only one story, the tale of God's search for the human race and of humankind's questioning of God) is an open-ended story, one that is incomplete until the reader has responded and entered into the drama. It is therefore a story of our time and of every time.

Fourthly the Bible is an encounter with "holy mystery", an irreplaceable aid, itself mysterious, in our journey towards the mystery that we call God.

God is, in the phrase of a modern theologian, a "radiant darkness", inviting us to journey into the mystery that we are and that God is, with our eyes open to all the evil and suffering that there is in God's creation, in our world and our time. It carries, however, the assurance that God is still working to make creation what it could be, to remove oppression. For evil and suffering and oppression are not the end of the story; God calls us into life and into fellowship (or communion) with each other. We read the Bible in the end because it gives meaning to all our struggles.

iv) A text for our times

I should like to end this book with the closing words of Matthew's gospel, which hint at why we still read the Bible today.

The Ending of the Holy Gospel according to Matthew

> *Now the eleven disciples journeyed to Galilee*
> *to the mountain which Jesus had decreed for them.*
> *And seeing him they worshipped; but some had doubts.*
>
> *And coming forward Jesus spoke to them saying:*
> *All authority in heaven and on earth is given to me.*
>
> *Therefore journey, make disciples of all nations/gentiles,*
> *baptising them in the name of the Father and of the Son*
> *and of the Holy Spirit,*
> *teaching them to keep all things that I have commanded you.*
>
> *And see I am with you all the days*
> *until the consummation of the world.*

The passage starts with the jarring "eleven", a reminder that one of the original twelve had not only turned traitor but also committed suicide. We live, the gospel is saying, in an as yet imperfect world, aptly described as "Galilee of the Gentiles". However, it is not a world without hope, as Matthew gently indicates by taking the eleven to a "mountain". It was on a mountain that Matthew had placed Jesus' central teaching about how to live out discipleship. Mountains, we remarked in the chapter on the beatitudes, are places where humans meet the divine.

But it is not an easy meeting, our encounter with the divine; it is filled with a dialectic between questioning and faith. Matthew expresses this splendidly in the laconic line: "and seeing him they worshipped", allowing that they (that is, we) have faith, and in the same breath pointing to their and our uncertainties: "but some doubted".

That is the way we humans are, and it is no earthly use denying or regretting it. In the end, as Matthew indicates, it is not on our authority that we get there: "all authority in heaven and onearth is given" to Jesus. So these doubting humans are given a job, namely to pass on the message to absolutely everyone in the world, incorporating them into the mystery in the name of the triune God. At this point Matthew makes it plain to us that he is not even pretending to talk about Jesus and the twelve, for it would have been impossible for Jesus to formulate this Trinitarian formula; this speech is set in the time of the Church, that is, in our time, the reader's time.

This becomes clearer in the final words of the gospel, which leap off the page into our country and this time. The gospel promises the presence of Jesus until creation is consumed in God's new creation. Jesus does not say "I will be with you"; the tense is present, and the promise is for all time, and with it we can end (though it is only a beginning) this account of what it is to read the Bible today:

> *And see I am with you all the days*
> *until the consummation of the world.*

Afterthought

There is always something of a gap between the completing of a manuscript and the appearance of a new book. The manuscript of this book was completed as South Africa waited, rather uneasily, for a "New South Africa" to appear, and the last lines of its first draft were written not long before April 27th 1994, when the elections were due to take place; but at that stage it was not at all clear that the elections would happen, or whether, especially in our part of the world, bloodshed could possibly be avoided.

And so we held our collective breath, and, astonishingly, the party that had been holding aloof from the process came in, and the elections happened, and April 27th is one of those days of which I am proud to be able to say "I was there". I had the good fortune to be a district observer for the election, and I drove the rounds of our electoral district, and saw the miracle happening. The word "miracle" is cheapened by over-use, but that is what we had, the power of God breaking into our world, and healing its wounds and breathing new life. It was there in the faces of the old Zulu women I saw hobbling to their vote in the chilly pre-dawn, and in the young police-persons who found themselves at the service of the community that day, and thoroughly enjoyed the experience, and in the extraordinary queues, up to four hours long in my district, where whites and blacks met on equal terms, and got to know each other, and then wondered why they had wasted so much time living apart. It was there in the feeling of liberation, not just of black people from oppression, but also of white people from the crippling burden of guilt; God was at work there, healing and mending and giving hope.

Nor was it a one-day wonder, for we are still living with the miracle and growing into it. There are of course still problems in South Africa, and it is easy enough to write "worst-case" scenarios, and to point to fault-lines along which the whole fragile unity might shatter. That, however, is the human condition: always there is the possibility of disaster, and always God invites the human race to act as collaborators in building the world that might be.

So I am constantly amazed and moved at the little thing that are signs of something new in this country: the generals saluting their new President on Inauguration Day, the unforced pride that most whites seem to feel in Nelson Mandela, the efforts of the SABC to learn and pronounce correctly the

African names mentioned in news reports, the South African Rugby team that did its best to learn the words of the beautiful hymn *Nkosi Sikelele iAfrika*, which not long ago was thought to be a communist anthem, the blossoming of friendships across racial boundaries, and, very dear indeed to my heart, the admiration among whites for non-white cricketers from India, Pakistan, and the West Indies. I could go on: naturally, these glimpses do not mean that all our problems are solved, or we should not need a Reconstruction and Development Programme; and I am not saying that there will be no disaster in this country, for there is always the possibility, wherever you are, that human selfishness and greed will wreak their awfulness.

Nevertheless, we did experience a miracle; it was so unexpected, and so absolutely right, that there is no other word for it. And it has not evaporated "like the morning dew"; it is still there, underpinning our struggles to build a just society. Why did it happen? The reasons are many and complex, and there were solid political and economic factors pointing in that direction. That, however, is visible to hindsight; before April 27th, it took a real act of faith to say "all shall be well and all manner of things shall be well". So I should like to suggest that a part of the reason for the miracle may be that a very large number of South Africans are Bible-reading Christians, who have therefore been unconsciously nurtured on the vision for our world, and the grasp of the essential unity of the human race, which lie in the Bible's pages. I cannot prove that, of course; it is not the kind of proposition that *can* be proved; nor can it be proved that there is a God who exists and who is at work in building a new South Africa. However I happen to believe that it is so.

And now we have moved beyond elections to the task of rebuilding, with sleeves rolled up and a generous heart. If these pages have had something to say about the relevance of the Bible to the South Africa that was laying down the burden of *apartheid* and taking up the challenge of elections, then, and by the same token, I think that they also have something to say about our present phase, of Reconstruction and Development. Nor is it good news for South Africa alone, for the Bible is rich in vision, and that vision is for any country in the world where the Kingdom of God is not yet built, which is to say, for any country in the world. So this book is not a political programme, nor anything like it, but a pointing back to the Bible, which speaks in tones of undying freshness to your country and your time.